T0131348

Jon Poole

Business Coaching

in easy steps

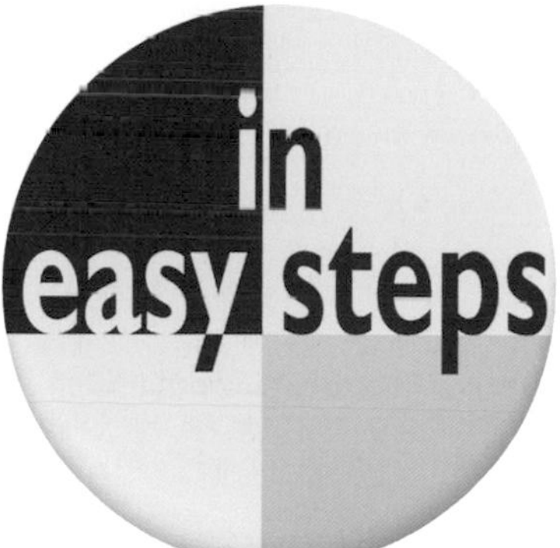

In easy steps is an imprint of In Easy Steps Limited
Southfield Road · Southam
Warwickshire CV47 0FB · United Kingdom
www.ineasysteps.com

Graham Gooch's photo credit
Kieran Galvin

In Easy Steps Limited supports The Forest Stewardship Council (FSC), the leading international forest certification organisation. All our titles that are printed on Greenpeace approved FSC certified paper carry the FSC logo.

Printed and bound in the United Kingdom

ISBN 978-1-84078-384-1

Contents

1 What is Coaching? 7

Coaching in Sport 8
The Coach in Business 10
Benefits of Coaching 11
Coaching Styles 12
Levels of Learning 14
What can be Coached? 15
To Coach or Not to Coach? 16
The Alternatives 17
Coaching Applications 18
Learning Stages 20
Summary 22

2 The Coaching Relationship 23

The Coach and Performer 24
The Coach's Role 25
The Manager as Coach 26
Understanding the Benefits 28
The Performer's Perspective 30
Measuring Success 31
Summary 32

3 Preparing to Coach 33

Choosing a Location 34
Coaching Off Site 35
Managing Interruptions 36
Timing 37
Body Language 38
Before the First Session 40
Summary 42

4 The Coaching Process 43

It's as Easy as A-B-C... 44
A is for... 46
The Benefits of Aspirations 48
Asking for Aspirations 49
B is for... 50
Asking for Building Blocks 51
Listing Them All 52
Focusing on One 53
C is for... 54
Getting the Detail 56
D is for... 58
More About Solutions 60
E is for... 62
Dealing with Blockages 64
The Next Meeting 65
F is for... 66
Summary 68

5 Supporting Skills 69

Questioning 70
Open and Closed Questions 71
High-gain Questions 72
Keeping it Conversational 74
Leading Questions 75
Questioning to Focus 76
More on Questioning 78
Listening 79
Body Language 80
Barriers to Listening 82
Active Listening 83
Reflecting 84
Summarizing Examples 85
Taking Notes 86
Mind Mapping 88
Summary 90

6 Setting Goals 91

Goals in Coaching 92
Why Set Goals? 93
Goal-setting Models 94
SMART 95
MARC and Other Derivatives 96
SMART in Coaching 97
Reactions to Goals 98
Personality and Goals 99
SMART in Sport? 100
Visualization 102
Using Visualization 104
Goal-setting Examples 106
Summary 108

7 Ongoing Coaching 109

Reviewing Progress 110
Transfer to the Real World 111
Reviewing Current 112
Dealing with Slow Progress 113
Changing Plans 114
The Next Building Block 115
Starting the Process Again 116
Follow-up Meeting Format 118
The Ongoing Relationship 120
Evaluating Progress 122
Evaluation in Practice 124
Observing Your Coachee 125
Summary 126

8 The Second Dimensions 127

About the 2nd Dimensions 128
The Coaching Environment 130
Using the 2nd Dimensions 132
Aspirations 134

Dealing with Differences 136
Building Blocks 138
Current 140
Development 142
Energize 144
Follow up 146
Putting it All Together 148
Summary 150

9 Coaching Applications 151

Self-Coaching 152
Mentoring 154
Business Consulting 156
More Business Consulting 158
Career Change 160
The External Coach 162
Remote Coaching 164
Bringing in Coaching 166
Embedding into the Culture 168
Difficult Scenarios 170
Some Final Tips 172

10 Next Steps 173

What Next? 174
Coach Yourself 176
Coaching Process 178
Development Actions Log 179
Development Actions List 180
Simple Analysis Tools 181
Transferable Skills 182
Values 183
Author's Website 184
Other Useful Websites 185
Further Reading 186

Index 187

1 What is Coaching?

The term 'coaching' is often used to describe any form of training. Before learning how to coach, you firstly need to understand what coaching is, how you can use it to maximise an individual's potential and the benefits to the individual and the organization.

8 Coaching in Sport

10 The Coach in Business

11 Benefits of Coaching

12 Coaching Styles

14 Levels of Learning

15 What can be Coached?

16 To Coach or Not to Coach?

17 The Alternatives

18 Coaching Applications

20 Learning Stages

22 Summary

Coaching in Sport

We are probably all familiar with the fact that top athletes and sports performers have coaches to help improve or maximize their performance, but do we know how they do what they do? How do they improve the performance of those they coach? Why, if they are so good, isn't the coach the one that is taking part and winning all the medals?

Hot tip 

If you coach a junior sports team, why not try practicing some of the skills you pick up from this book on them?

At the level most sports people are assigned a coach they are probably already well beyond the point where they need to learn basic skills or techniques. They may already be performing at the very highest level in their field of sport and could even be the world's number one in their chosen sport.

Coaching to stay on top

At the point when an athlete sets a new world record or wins a major championship, does he or she sack the coach because there is nothing else to learn? Of course not – at this point the coach is probably of even more benefit to the performer.

Getting to the top may have been an incredible achievement but staying at the top can be an even bigger challenge. Once a performer has set a new standard of excellence there will undoubtedly be others close on their heels looking to better that achievement. By continually looking at areas to refine and improve, the coach can work with the performer to stay at the top for longer.

The role of a coach

The coach has a critical role to play, supporting the performer and helping them to develop their full potential. Through effective and structured questioning techniques the coach can:

- Help the performer to focus on areas of performance that are going to make a difference
- Act as a sounding board for the performer's new ideas
- Provide independent feedback on performance
- Help the performer to become more self-aware
- Praise and encourage when they see improvements
- Test and challenge the performer's thinking
- Provide encouragement if things don't go so well

Not telling or selling

What you will note from this list is that it doesn't include 'tell the performer what to do'. This is the first critical lesson of coaching. It is not 'telling', 'advising' or, for that matter, 'selling' your views. It is about questioning to encourage the performer to focus their thinking so that they determine and act upon their own solutions.

Sports coach or instructor?

Quite often in sport you will hear the terms 'instructor' and 'coach' used indiscriminately. We tend to talk about a ski instructor but refer to a football or basketball coach. As you will realize, the term 'coach' as we will be using it in this book has a very specific meaning and should not be confused with the roles played by many who are really trainers or instructors.

Coaching is a very different activity to instructing or training and uses different skills and techniques.

The mind game

Most top sports people who are competing at the highest level are likely to be concentrating less on developing basic skills and more on the psychology of their performance. What makes the difference between a good performer and the very best is often more about what is going on in the performer's mind.

The coach can help the performer by ensuring they approach their sport with a positive and focused mindset, eliminating any thoughts they may have of failure.

The Coach in Business

Although the environments may seem very different, the role of the coach in the business environment is very similar to that of the coach in the world of sport. The business coach is still interested in getting the very best performance from the individual – whether the business performer is a sales person, a creative writer, a finance manager or a company director.

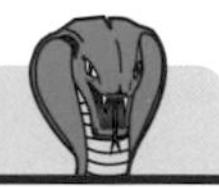

Beware

Don't be tempted to come up with the goals for your performer. We will see how beneficial it is to get them to come up with their own goals.

Different coaching goals

Of course the skills being focused on in the business context are most likely going to be very different, as are the outcomes. Instead of having the goal of becoming a world record holder in the javelin or achieving a personal best in the high jump, the goals may be to successfully manage a first IT project, achieve this year's sales target or to become an effective delegator.

The coach as manager

Quite often the coach in business is also the individual's manager and clearly this is a different situation to most sports coaches who are often independent from the performer's manager.

The enhanced relationship developed through coaching can be very helpful in terms of the day-to-day management of an individual and is one of the key benefits of using coaching. This is something we will be exploring later in this book.

Benefits of Coaching

Coaching, when carried out effectively, is one of the most powerful ways to enhance an individual's personal effectiveness. Often it has many benefits over more traditional methods of development such as training courses, workshops or direct instruction.

Because the coach is using probing questioning to draw out solutions from the performer, we will see that it:

- Enables the performer to better understand themselves through challenging questioning and also helps them to focus on the most important things
- Allows the coach to gain a better understanding of the performer which can result in a better working relationship between the two
- Leaves the responsibility for development with the performer which can lead them to be more motivated to achieve their desired outcomes
- Gives the performer confidence to tackle this and other issues – once they have the correct mindset they can apply this thinking to a range of other situations
- Provides more focused development in specific areas rather than providing one-size-fits-all solutions
- Encourages more creative and personalized solutions which are based on the individual's needs
- Ultimately leads to real and lasting improvement in the performer's performance

No need to be an expert

Drawing solutions from the performer also means that the coach does not have to be as knowledgeable or skilful as the performer in the subject being coached. Some level of understanding of the topic can sometimes be helpful but the coach's role is to help the performer to determine their own solutions, not to come up with all the answers.

This explains why a coach doesn't necessarily need to be as good as or better than the performer. They just need to be an excellent coach.

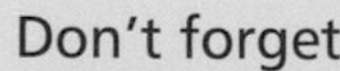

You don't have to be an expert in the topic being coached – you just have to be an excellent coach.

Coaching Styles

Before looking at coaching in detail we need to firstly provide some background on coaching styles. Coaching styles follow the same principles as those used for leadership. Examining these will help to ensure you adopt the most effective style when coaching.

Leadership styles

As managers we must choose our leadership style to suit the situation and the experience of the individual – this is a well established concept. At one extreme we can choose to use a directive or 'tell' approach and, at the other, an empowering or hands-off style. The following diagram describes this and under what circumstances each may be appropriate:

If you are interested in finding out more about leadership styles, refer to Chapter 10 for some additional resources on the subject.

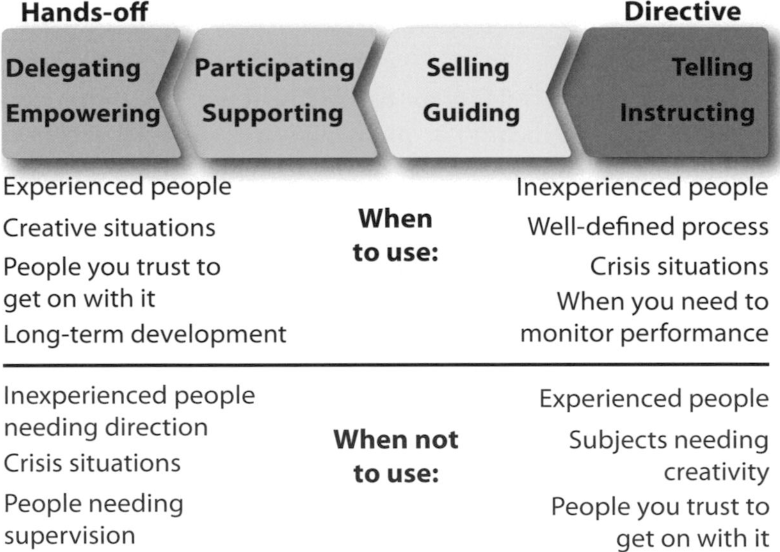

A style for all situations

You will realize from this diagram there are no right or wrong styles of leadership but that some styles just suit certain situations better than others. Conversely there are some styles which are less appropriate and even unhelpful in certain situations.

Although the diagram describes the styles at each end of the leadership spectrum, you should note this is a continuous scale. There are also many other styles of leadership you can adopt to suit situations around the middle ground where less monitoring and instruction is needed and where supporting becomes helpful.

Adapting your style

Everyone has a dominant style of leadership – one which they will normally tend to adopt. This only becomes a problem if a manager only ever uses this one style. It may be a very appropriate style for most situations and with certain individuals but, occasionally, this style could actually be unhelpful or even demotivating. For example, telling a highly competent and experienced person precisely how to do a task could be very demotivating and even patronizing.

The trick is identifying your dominant style and then learning to be flexible enough to adapt your approach to any of the other styles when faced with a situation that requires it.

Don't forget

We all have a dominant leadership style but must also learn to adopt other styles when the situation requires it.

Coaching style

In most cases coaching is used to enhance or refine skills or behaviors the performer is already familiar with and is most likely already using. These skills may have been acquired through traditional training, have been self-taught or learnt through trial and error. Where your performer is experienced in the subject you will normally be able to adopt a coaching style towards the hands-off and empowering end of the style spectrum.

Hands-off coaching style

Here are some other reasons why, when coaching, you will normally be able to adopt a hands-off style:

- As well as already having some level of experience, your performer is also hopefully someone who you can trust to work without having to be continually pushed or monitored
- Some of the solutions you will want to encourage your performer to come up with may require some creativity rather than relying on your own tried and tested solutions
- Most areas you will be looking to coach are ones that will benefit from long-term solutions rather than quick fixes

Using a hands-off coaching style means questioning your performer to help them focus on priority areas. It also means encouraging them to come up with their own solutions rather than telling them what to do and encouraging them to set and monitor their own goals – this is far more motivating for your performer.

Levels of Learning

Another important concept to understand before getting into the detail of coaching is the relationship between knowledge, skills and behaviors and how coaching impacts each of these different levels of learning. To illustrate each we will take as a scenario the activity of learning to drive a car.

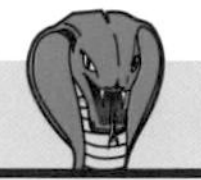

Beware

Just because someone learns the theory doesn't necessarily mean that they can apply that knowledge. They must still develop the skills to become proficient.

Knowledge

Before even thinking about driving for the first time there is a certain amount of information we need to know. This may be very basic knowledge such as: What do each of the pedals do? How do I turn on the ignition? What is the difference between the hand brake and the foot brake? What are the rules of the road? All of this is background knowledge that will help us when we try to actually drive.

Skills

Just because we have learnt the necessary knowledge, however, does not automatically make us skilled drivers. So, having acquired the necessary knowledge, we then need to learn how to apply this knowledge by learning the skills to drive. Skills require application and practice and cannot therefore be learnt by merely reading about them.

Behaviors

Interestingly, people all start by learning the same knowledge and practicing roughly the same skills but over time people then develop their own behaviors. There are people who drive carefully, others more aggressively and some without a care in the world. It is important to note that some behaviors can positively support our skills and lead to better performance whereas others may have a negative impact on our performance of these skills.

What can be Coached?

As we have already stated, coaching is particularly useful as a way of refining or further developing existing skills or behaviors. Given that coaching is normally based on an ongoing relationship or series of meetings, it lends itself to areas of development where long-lasting change is required or where development is best tackled gradually over a period of time. For this reason coaching is particularly useful for areas such as:

- Assertiveness and confidence
- Influencing
- Effective questioning and listening
- Thinking strategically
- Creating a balance between work and personal lives
- Sales behaviors and skills
- Personal organization or time management

Take the first example in the above list. Very few people would expect that by attending a single training course or workshop on the subject of confidence their deep-seated lack of confidence would be transformed forever – however good the course was.

Hot tip

If faced with someone with a long-term development issue don't just put them on a training course – think about coaching them instead.

Long term solution

A course is likely to be attended by a number of delegates and therefore any solutions are going to be broad-brush and not specific to an individual. Furthermore, it is unlikely that a single event will turn around behaviors and thinking habits, which may have built up over a number of years, without ongoing support and reinforcement only really possible through regular and ongoing coaching.

Ongoing relationship

An important distinction between coaching and any other form of training is that it is not a one-off event. It is an ongoing process where the coach and performer can progressively work on one or a number of focused areas of personal development.

The number of coaching sessions needed will vary but could spread over several weeks, months or even years in some cases depending on the issue being coached.

To Coach or Not to Coach?

More focused development

If you have ever scanned through brochures offering training courses or workshops you will see that the subjects covered are relatively broad. They are generally designed to appeal to a wide range of potential delegates looking for broad-based training on a given subject.

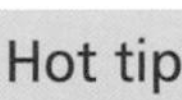

Hot tip

Experienced employees who have been on all the training courses will find coaching far more useful for developing their specific needs.

Coaching, on the other hand, allows the individual to focus on very specific development issues. This can be far more effective, especially for more experienced people who may have attended all the usual courses and do not want to waste a whole day to learn just one or two specific skills.

When not to coach

Having considered the benefits of coaching and how useful it is for so many situations we need to look at the few occasions where coaching may not be an appropriate approach to take.

In a crisis

When a short-term or instant solution is required it may be necessary to use other, more directive management solutions. For instance, if you were to discover a fire in a building it would not be the time to coach another individual into finding new, personalized solutions for getting out of the building! A simple, directive instruction would be far more effective.

Coaching knowledge

Coaching as a means to acquire knowledge may not necessarily be the best option. For example, you may need to help an individual to understand about the internal structure of a computer. You could try asking your performer to come up with their own thoughts on, say, the workings of a microprocessor but, unless they know something about electronics in the first place, they will be merely guessing.

What is possible through coaching is to help an individual to determine *how* they are going to best find out and learn this information – coaching them in the skill of learning.

The Alternatives

Learning knowledge

We have just highlighted that coaching is not necessarily the solution for every development situation. Knowledge can be best acquired through a number of means. For example:

- Reading management or technical books or following a course of distance learning
- Searching the internet
- Attending lectures on the chosen subject

Group learning

There are also times where core skills are best learned by being part of a group in a 'classroom' environment. This provides the opportunity to learn alongside others and discuss a subject together. It may also help where consistency of a specific methodology is important across an organization.

Poor performance

There will be other occasions where coaching may not be an appropriate solution. Regrettably some behavior or poor performance issues may, ultimately need to be dealt with through formal disciplinary action – particularly if the behavior is disruptive and the individual is not in a mindset to want to engage in coaching.

Coaching or counseling?

If you are already familiar with the concepts of counseling then you may be wondering what the difference is between coaching and counseling. Counseling is also a way of drawing out solutions from an individual without imposing them – helping and supporting the performer in making their own decisions.

Many of the skills are, indeed, very similar. One key difference is that coaching is more focused on a performance outcome, often related to work and life issues whereas counseling is more focused on psychological healing.

On a few occasions you may find that the coaching discussion strays more towards counseling. As a coach you need to understand the limitations of your skill-base. Where necessary, you may need to suggest that the person you are coaching seeks alternative help for their counseling need.

Beware 

If your coaching starts to turn into counseling you may need to stop and recommend they seek alternative help with a counselor.

Coaching Applications

On the following two pages we have provided more detailed examples where coaching can provide real benefit. Whilst this book focuses on business coaching we have also provided an example to show how coaching can be used very effectively in non-work situations. There are clearly many more applications:

Hot tip 

Coaching someone to get clarity over their career direction can be very helpful. We look at this in more detail in Chapter 9.

Business applications

- **Career development** – Supporting and developing an individual through their career is an ideal application for coaching. It can be used in the first place to help an individual get clarity over their overall career direction. Then regular ongoing coaching meetings can be used to support their development as they progress in their career.

- **Delegation** – The theory behind delegation is relatively straightforward but putting this into practice can sometimes lead to problems, particularly for newly appointed managers. New managers can feel awkward about having to delegate work for the first time (often to those who were previously their peers). Coaching can help to explore what lies behind their concerns and provide practical actions and regular support to help them build their confidence.

- **Managing meetings** – Standard courses on the subject of managing meetings provide a good theoretical grounding in the skills needed to run effective meetings. Putting these into practice requires the use of a number of supporting behaviors including personal organization, assertiveness, decision making and open-mindedness. All are behaviors that can be developed and supported through regular coaching with feedback from real meetings.

- **Selling** – There are possibly more training materials available on selling skills than any other business subject. Experienced salespeople will have been on many sales training programmes and as a result are unlikely to gain much from 'refresher' training. As with many activities, the mindset of the individual can also play a significant role in their success. Coaching allows you to explore with a salesperson very specific areas and create solutions focused on the precise needs of the individual.

- **Personal organization** – Many people struggle with what is often referred to as 'time management'. In reality it could be a number of specific issues from poor organization, ineffective delegation, or a reluctance to say 'no' when over-worked. Solutions often require considerable coaching and support until new good habits become the natural way of doing things.

- **Negotiation** – The skills and tactics needed for negotiation can be learned through training but to be effective under the pressures of a real situation requires a number of supporting behaviors such as emotional control, tenacity and heightened communication skills. Coaching is an ideal way to support and develop someone in these behaviors.

Non-work applications

- **Quitting smoking or drinking** – These are just two examples of activities for which coaching can play a part in trying to control or alter long-term and deep-seated habits. Clearly, where an individual has persistent or medical related issues, you should not interfere with any professional help they are seeking. Where, however, an individual chooses to cut down or stop their habit, you can play a vital role in helping them through coaching on a regular basis.

Hot tip

Coaching is a good way to tackle people's long-term habits. However, you should not expect instant results – you may need to provide coaching support for many months.

Learning Stages

We have already described the relationship between knowledge, skills and behaviors so finally in this chapter we will look briefly at a model which explains how people acquire skills and behaviors. This will be useful, not only so you can understand the progress of your performer's development but also so that, as you learn to become an effective coach, you can appreciate your own development stages towards becoming a fully competent coach.

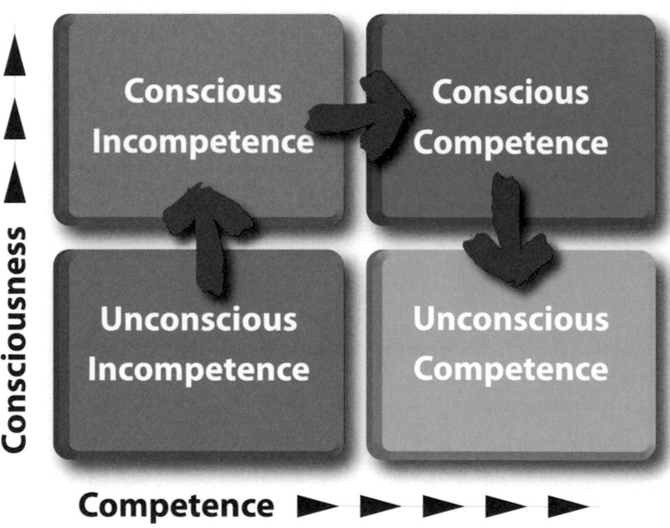

As you will see, the skill development path breaks down into four stages. To illustrate each, we are going to turn, again, to our earlier example of learning to drive.

Unconsciously incompetent

In this first stage, a learner is incapable of performing a skill but is also unconscious of what is required to perform the skill – they won't even be aware that they can't do it.

In terms of learning to drive, at an early age most children won't have any knowledge of what is really required to drive a car. They may watch adults driving but will not have any real comprehension of the background knowledge we described earlier such as the rules of the road or how to operate the controls.

An important point to note about this stage is that, unless an individual becomes aware of their incapability, they will have no motivation to do anything about it.

Unless someone is aware of their lack of capability they will not be motivated to change.

Consciously incompetent

This second stage of development occurs once the learner has understood the skills needed to perform a task but has not yet learned to use them.

When someone shows an interest in learning to drive, they may become more aware of the complexities of driving but they will not have had any lessons and are therefore still incapable. By reading and asking questions a learner picks up the background knowledge but has no experience of using the required skills.

Consciously competent

This stage is reached when the learner first starts to practice using the new skills. They are able to perform the skills but are very conscious of what they are doing and still need to focus their attention on getting them right.

In our learning to drive example, the learner is now physically driving the car – maybe having lessons – but everything is still awkward and mechanistic. They will be very conscious, for instance, of their hands and feet and which pedals they need to press and when.

When a learner reaches this stage it is important that they don't give up just because everything feels awkward. Regular practice will take the learner to the next stage.

Hot tip 

Don't worry if a learner feels awkward when first using a new skill – this will become more natural with practice.

Unconsciously competent

This is arguably the ideal state in terms of developing a skill as the individual is now capable of performing the skill and without even having to consciously think about it.

If you are an experienced driver you will recognise this state if you have ever driven whilst deep in thought and, having reached your destination, found you have almost no recollection of the journey. You will have been using your driving skills unconsciously!

We describe this as 'arguably' the ideal state because this last level of unconsciousness can lead to complacency. If you interact with others whilst giving no conscious consideration to your actions you are unlikely to be performing at your best. You should ideally have sufficient experience to apply the appropriate skills or behaviors unconsciously but still maintain a level of consciousness to ensure you are fully in control of how you apply them.

Summary

- Coaching in sport and in business is very similar – in both, the coach is trying to help the performer to maximise their potential
- A coach can help by providing support, encouragement, motivation and, above all, focus
- The role of the coach is to encourage the performer, through effective questioning, to think through their own solutions rather than to tell or advise them what to do
- As leaders, we all have a dominant leadership style. Whatever our leadership style, it is important to realize there are other styles which are sometimes more appropriate
- When coaching, the most used style is hands-off. This will empower the performer and ensure they remain motivated towards their personal development
- Coaching is an ideal way of enhancing existing skills and behaviors
- Coaching is generally an ongoing engagement and therefore lends itself to development needs requiring longer-term solutions
- Coaching should not be seen as the only development solution – there are times when other solutions may be more suitable
- The coach does not need to be as skilful as the performer, but they do need to be competent as a coach
- Coaching can help to strengthen the relationship between the performer and the manager
- It is difficult to use coaching to develop knowledge directly but it can be used to help someone develop the skills necessary to acquire knowledge
- If a subject is best handled by counseling know your limitations and, if necessary, recommend they seek counseling

2 The Coaching Relationship

The person you are coaching should enter into coaching with a positive mindset. They need to believe in the coach, the process and how coaching will benefit them.

24 The Coach and Performer

25 The Coach's Role

26 The Manager as Coach

28 Understanding the Benefits

30 The Performer's Perspective

31 Measuring Success

32 Summary

The Coach and Performer

Hot tip

Take an honest look at your interactions with your team. What levels of responsibility do you currently give them?

You will have already realized that the performer needs to play a very active role in the coaching relationship. The responsibility for choosing the areas for development, coming up with possible development solutions and the motivation to make it happen should ideally all rest with the performer.

On receive

It is vital that the individual enters into the coaching relationship with a positive mindset. They need to believe in the process, in you as their coach, and also understand how coaching will ultimately benefit them.

To describe this positive mindset we sometimes refer to it as the performer being 'on receive' – that is, open-minded and wanting to play an active part in the process and relationship.

Explaining roles

When you first introduce coaching it is worth spending some time explaining about coaching and how it works. At this early stage it will be helpful to get your performer in this receptive mindset by describing:

- The nature of your role as a hands-off coach
- Their responsibilities as performer

You can explain that you will be expecting them to do a lot of the thinking and decision-making. If your performer has not previously been accustomed to taking this level of responsibility they may need some encouragement to do this initially.

The Coach's Role

Adding value as coach

It may seem, from what has been described so far, that as coach, you don't have much of a part to play in this relationship. What difference are you making if all the control and choice rests with your performer? The answer is that you are playing a vital role by:

- Asking the right questions
- Challenging and testing your performer's responses (but not criticizing or judging)
- Helping to focus the mindset of your performer

Remember, you don't need to be as knowledgeable or as skilful as your performer. In fact, sometimes it helps not to know too much about the topic being coached as this will discourage you from providing direct advice or instruction.

Openness and honesty

Coaching can only work if the performer is prepared to be open and honest over their responses when questioned or challenged. The old adage 'garbage in, garbage out' certainly applies to coaching. The more engaged the performer is in the coaching process and the more honest they are with their responses, the more they are likely to get out of it.

There is little point in going through the pretence of a coaching session where the performer is giving you false answers or responses which they think you want to hear.

Confidentiality

The performer will only feel prepared to be open and honest with their responses – particularly to sensitive questions about their performance or their personal feelings – if you have their complete trust.

They must be reassured that any information discussed whilst being coached will be treated sensitively and discreetly and that nothing of what is discussed is going to be divulged outside of the coaching meetings.

Beware

Make sure you don't inadvertently disclose any information obtained during your coaching sessions.

The Manager as Coach

Trust

As we have already mentioned, coaching can provide some real benefits in terms of helping to build a closer relationship between you and the person you are coaching. If the relationship between the two of you is not good in the first place, forcing an individual to accept coaching is not going to work.

Trust is not something that can be turned on and off when needed. A healthy and trusting working relationship is normally something which is built up over a long period of time and can be knocked back very easily.

Beware 

You can't engender trust overnight. If trust is a problem with someone you want to coach, stop and deal with this first.

Current relationship

It is useful, before entering into a coaching relationship, to give some careful consideration to the quality of your relationship with the individual you are intending to coach. Be honest with yourself and note the way that the individual normally interacts with you. If you know or sense there is any lack of trust it may be better to spend more time laying the groundwork by trying to establish a firmer relationship before even contemplating coaching.

Conflict of interest

There may be a few occasions where a conflict of interest arises making it difficult for you to act as the coach. For example, where an individual you are coaching applies for a new role or for promotion and you are on the judging panel, you cannot expect the candidate to open up their innermost thoughts or provide an honest self-appraisal about their skill-gaps in a coaching session.

In this situation it may be best to either suspend the coaching until after the decision has been made or suggest someone else acts as their coach if you have not yet started.

Dangers of taking over

Your role is to empower the individual, encouraging them to take personal responsibility for their own development.

As their coach, you should not take over responsibility. If you try to take control by thinking through the performer's issues for them and also try to determine what the solutions should be, then there is a strong possibility that the coaching will fail because:

- The performer may not agree with your view of the issue
- The performer may not agree with your view of their current performance
- Development solutions you come up with may not be ones the performer is comfortable with or prepared to commit to
- Goals that you set are likely to feel imposed and may lead to the performer resisting or just giving up
- The performer will not get used to the idea of determining solutions for themselves which they can apply when dealing with other situations
- As a result of all of the above, the performer is unlikely to be motivated to improve

Giving the performer the responsibility

If, on the other hand, you encourage the performer to appraise themselves, they must surely believe in their own assessment of themselves and their performance. If they come up with their own ideas to develop themselves, they are only likely to come up with ideas or solutions which appeal to them and that they will be prepared to pursue.

Benefits beyond coaching

Ultimately, if you encourage your performer to develop a mindset where they automatically think through issues for themselves, they will start to become far more confident when needing to tackle other issues both within coaching and in their broader work life.

Instead of coming to you with problems which they expect you to sort out, they will start coming with solutions and this will surely make your role as a manager much easier.

Hot tip

Become more aware of your interactions with those who work for you. If you notice yourself taking over, stop yourself and instead ask them for their views.

Don't forget

If you start to encourage others to come to you with solutions or ideas it will make your job so much easier.

Understanding the Benefits

In the business environment it is usual for an organization to expect that coaching an individual will have some performance benefit or payback to the organization. After all, the organization is investing time and possibly money in providing the coaching.

Hot tip

Put yourself in the performer's shoes and think about how you would feel if you were approached by your boss to be coached.

Win-win

Of course the best situation is if the individual and the organization both benefit.

Benefits to the individual:

- Receiving personal attention leading to better motivation
- Improvement in performance or widening of their skill-base
- Personal growth in their role or even promotion

Benefits to the organization:

- A more motivated employee
- Increased performance from employee
- Ultimately an improvement in bottom-line performance

Direct benefit

The business benefit resulting from coaching may be very clear and easily identifiable. This would certainly be the case when coaching to enhance, say, the selling skills of a key salesperson.

An improvement in selling skills or behaviors should lead to an increase in personal sales and in turn help to achieve the overall objectives of the business.

Less direct benefits

On some occasions, the link may be less easy to identify. For instance, an organization may decide to support an individual who is looking to improve their work/life balance through coaching.

There is still a positive benefit to the organization because ultimately, if the individual improves their work/life balance, they are more likely to feel motivated and refreshed when they are at work. This, in turn, should lead to greater productivity.

The topic you coach may only have an indirect benefit to the organization.

This second example, and many others like it, are more difficult to measure or to ascertain the benefit to the business. But providing you can determine a link, there is no reason why you should not provide coaching around this subject.

Balancing objectives

If you try to impose a coaching objective on an individual and they cannot see the benefit to them, there is a danger that the individual will resist or not wish to engage. This needs to be balanced with the alternative scenario where an individual is given a completely free rein to pursue their own objectives or area of development.

In some situations this may be acceptable, but how will you react if your performer decides that they want you to focus their coaching sessions towards trying to lower their golf handicap!

Discussing beforehand

It is always helpful to discuss the organization's expectations, if there are any, with your performer before starting to coach. An acceptable compromise may be for the organization to set the broad parameters in which they want the coaching to focus and then leave the performer the scope to decide how, specifically, they will tackle it.

For instance, you may want to focus your performer on improving their productivity. Having set this broad parameter, they may decide to tackle this by focussing on their levels of motivation or alternatively, their personal organization skills.

The Performer's Perspective

WIIFM

As we have already highlighted, in most cases successful coaching will result in benefits for both the organization and the individual.

It helps to highlight the benefits to the performer right from the start. From the performer's perspective, they will want to know 'what's in it for me?' – often referred to as 'WIIFM'.

If the performer is clear what's in it for them they are likely to be far more committed to the process and therefore more likely to engage in coaching with an 'on-receive' mindset.

Don't sell

If you try selling the benefits of coaching to your performer they may feel they are being pushed into it. It is far better to ask them how they see coaching benefiting them and see how they respond.

Singling out

When you first start coaching you will probably want to try it out with one or two people first before extending to others. When you do this you will need to make it clear why you have picked them. You may choose an individual for a number of reasons:

- Someone you believe will respond well to coaching
- A high performer you want to give additional attention to
- A poor performer who has some clear areas for improvement

These may all be legitimate reasons for choosing someone but be careful that coaching doesn't become labelled as only something you do for poor performers or just for the 'elite'.

Beware 

People will be reluctant to come forward for coaching if they think it is only targeted at poor performers.

Measuring Success

Evaluation

It may seem odd to be considering the evaluation of coaching before you have even started but considering what and how you will evaluate a series of coaching sessions with an individual can help you and your performer to determine what the focus needs to be for the whole process.

Keeping on track

Having clarity from the outset over how you will determine whether the coaching has been a success will also help to keep both you and performer on track.

Without giving thought to what will constitute success there is every possibility the coaching will drift off course. It will also be difficult to know when the coaching has achieved its desired outcome and therefore when to stop.

Taking our example on page 28 of the business benefits resulting from the increase in the value of annual sales, it should be relatively easy to agree a measure that will indicate that the coaching is working. On the other hand, measuring whether someone's work/life balance is now as they want it to be may be far more difficult to evaluate.

Ask your performer

One question to ask at the start is: "How will you know when you have got there?" This is a very simple question which allows your performer to describe, in their own words, what will be a satisfactory conclusion to the coaching.

Keep it simple

However you decide to measure progress and ultimate success, don't try to make it too complicated. In most cases you should be able to determine success without having to put in place elaborate systems and measurement tools.

Measurable outcomes

As we will discuss in more detail later in this book under the subject of goal setting, it is not acceptable to have as a response: "My sales will improve". This is not measurable. How much improvement would you expect to see if the coaching is to be deemed a success?

Hot tip

Keep measures simple otherwise you will end up spending too much time measuring and not enough time coaching.

Summary

- The responsibility for generating ideas and development solutions should rest with the performer and not the coach
- It is normally useful to discuss the roles of coach and performer before starting, especially if this is the first time you have coached the individual
- The performer needs to enter a coaching relationship in a positive mindset – where they come as a willing participant. This is known as being 'on-receive'
- Even though, as coach, you are not coming up with all the answers you are still adding value through asking questions and keeping your performer focused
- It is important that the performer trusts the coach. If trust is not there in the first place you may need to work for some time to build it before commencing coaching
- If you foresee a potential conflict of interest you may need to postpone the coaching or suggest that someone else takes on the performer
- It is expected that there should be a business focus and benefit from the coaching and this is something which you can discuss with the performer before starting
- Ask the performer how they see the coaching benefiting them so they determine the WIIFM themselves. Having a clear understanding of how it will benefit them will ensure they are motivated and willing to actively participate
- Agree at the beginning how success will be measured as this will help you both to know when the coaching has succeeded
- Some coaching topics are easier to evaluate than others but normally, provided there is a business benefit, they are still worth coaching
- If you have to single out one or two people for coaching then think carefully about the impact of this on the performer and explain honestly why you have chosen them

3 Preparing to Coach

Preparing yourself and ensuring you have given careful thought to the location and other arrangements, before coaching, is essential.

34 Choosing a Location
35 Coaching Off Site
36 Managing Interruptions
37 Timing
38 Body Language
40 Before the First Session
42 Summary

Choosing a Location

Your choice of location and the environment for coaching can make a big difference in terms of the effectiveness of your coaching sessions. Given the sensitivity of the subjects that you are likely to be discussing, your coaching sessions need to be conducted in a confidential location, preferably free from noise and distractions. If you work in an open-plan environment, trying to find somewhere to meet for coaching can be difficult.

Beware

Using your office may seem a convenient option but can seem threatening to the performer and you may find it more difficult to avoid distractions.

Your office

Conducting the coaching sessions in your office, assuming you have an office, may seem an obvious choice but may not necessarily be the best option. Those that work for you may see your office as your 'territory'.

Depending on your leadership style and the relationship you already have with your performer, your office may not make them feel relaxed.

Other meeting rooms

Staff rooms or other common areas may be possible alternatives but will only be suitable if you can be sure that no one is likely to interrupt or be able to overhear your discussion.

If your organization has small rooms that can be booked for meetings these are probably an ideal choice. They will be seen as neutral ground and will ensure the right level of privacy.

Coaching Off Site

Away from the office

If you don't have access to internal meeting rooms, you could consider using a meeting room within a hotel or other local venue. This has the advantages of being a neutral place to meet and away from the office with all of its distractions. Of course there will probably be a cost associated with using such an option.

Using cafés

It may even be possible to conduct the coaching in a local café, hotel foyer or other similar public venue. Whilst this may not appear to be the most private arrangement, provided you can find a table that is relatively secluded, any noise from those around you is likely to drown out your conversation and should mean you are not easily overheard.

Of course, this would not be suitable if you anticipate needing to have a particularly sensitive discussion.

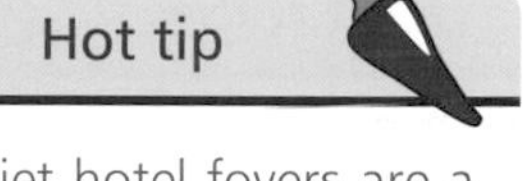

Quiet hotel foyers are a good option if you don't have a meeting room. It saves hiring a room and will probably just cost you a few coffees.

Restaurants

These are generally locations to avoid. Trying to conduct a coaching session over a meal is not the most conducive arrangement. There are likely to be too many interruptions – having to place your order, the meal and drinks being served, all the items on the table – all of which are likely to spoil the flow of the discussion. Both of you will find it difficult to maintain concentration levels with so many distractions.

Managing Interruptions

As with any confidential meetings such as selection interviews or performance appraisal meetings, it is important to ensure you are not interrupted during the coaching meeting. Here are some steps you can take to help you manage potential interruptions:

- Book more time in your diary than you need so you don't have to rush to try to finish towards the end of the meeting
- Put your phone and cell phone on divert or at least onto silent. Also ask your performer to do the same
- If using your office, mute any audible alarm on your computer which indicates new emails
- Ensure you tell others, including peers or your boss, you are not to be interrupted
- Put up a 'do not disturb' sign on your door
- Conduct the meetings off site
- Don't use the coaching meeting to discuss day-to-day business issues or get diverted from coaching during the meeting
- If the door to the room has a glass window, cover this over so that others can't see in

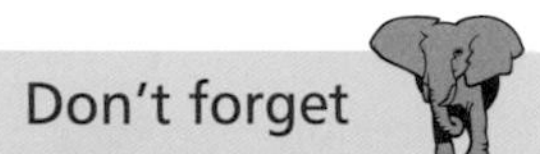

Switch off your cell phone or put it on silent and remind your performer to do the same before you start.

Undivided attention

It is important that your performer knows they have your undivided attention. If they sense that you would prefer to be getting on with something else or you seem distracted by other issues, it could undermine the session and your coaching relationship.

Watch your watch

Although it is important for you to keep a track of time, it can be very off-putting if you have to reach out your hand to look at your watch to see the time. It may come across that you are becoming impatient or bored.

An easy solution is to take your watch off at the start of the meeting and lay it in front of you. That way you are able to see how the time is going at a glance.

Put your watch on the desk in front of you so that you can easily keep a track of time.

Timing

Allow sufficient time

It is difficult to judge before you start coaching how much time you will need to set aside. It is better to err on the side of caution and allow more time than you think you will need. It can spoil the flow of a meeting if either of you become conscious you are running out of time and so start rushing.

Of course, if you do end up finishing earlier than the allotted time, you will at least have some valuable spare time to be able to get on with other work.

Hot tip

Allow more time in your diary than you think you will need to avoid running short of time.

Longer first meeting

As you will realize when we look at the coaching process in more detail, the first coaching session you conduct with an individual is likely to take longer than most subsequent meetings.

At the start of the initial meeting you will need to set the scene, agree how you are going to work together and also describe the process and your respective roles. It is at this first meeting that you will also discuss and agree with your performer the main focus of the coaching and this can take some time.

Timing guide

You can certainly expect a first meeting to last longer than an hour and maybe closer to two hours. Subsequent meetings are more likely to be shorter and some may be literally five to ten minutes on occasions.

If you run over

If you do run short of time it is best not to rush to get to the end. Agree to keep going at the current pace and at the end agree a time to meet again to finish off the discussion. Make sure you take notes because you will need to start the next meeting with a brief summary of what has been discussed so far.

Body Language

Body language – also sometimes referred to as 'non-verbal communication' – can play an important part in coaching. This is the communication we make or subtle signals we transmit in addition to merely the words we say. These include:

- Our gestures, body positions and facial expressions
- What we wear
- Our tone of voice ...but also...
- The environment which we create or operate within

Often the impact that body language can have on our communication can be more significant than the words we use.

As we work though this book we will highlight areas where body language could potentially have a significant effect on your coaching meetings.

Don't forget

When interacting with others whether at work or at home, your body language can have as much of an impact as the words you say.

Non-threatening environment

It is important to give some thought to the layout of the room or office you are planning on using – even before the first meeting takes place.

As we have already described with regards to the choice of meeting room, it is important that your performer feels relaxed. They should not be made to feel threatened or that you, as coach, are looking to control the meetings.

Seating

Where possible, seating should be on the same level and preferably informal. It can appear threatening if the performer is being looked down upon by a coach who is sitting in a higher or more formal chair.

Avoid having chairs facing opposite each other as this can also appear threatening.

Desk as a barrier

There is normally no need for the meeting to be conducted across a desk unless there are no alternatives. Again, avoid having chairs facing each other – having a desk as a barrier with chairs on opposite sides of the desk can come across as confrontational.

Desk corners

If you do find that you need to conduct the meeting at a desk, it is better to position the chairs on the same side of the desk or across a corner.

Hot tip

Just moving chairs to the same side of a desk instead of opposite each other can appear much less confrontational.

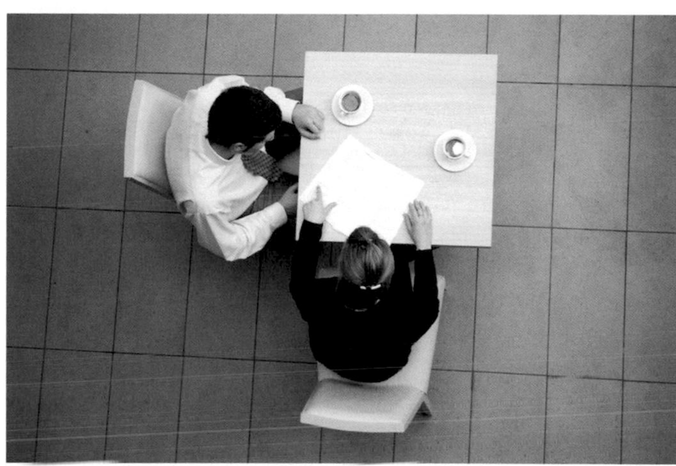

Changing your style

If your normal management style is relatively strict or formal and you suddenly change this to a relaxed style for coaching it could come across as contrived and not genuine.

It is therefore a good idea to take a look at your management style to work out how you are perceived by your team:

- Are you seen as directing or dominating?
- Are you generally approachable?
- Are people encouraged to come to you with ideas?

Office layout

What does your office and its layout say about your leadership style? Consider adapting your style, not just for your coaching sessions but as part of your day-to-day interactions with others.

Before the First Session

Planning the first session

If this is the first time you have coached a particular individual you will initially need to provide them with some information about coaching.

Based on what we have covered so far, here are some of the things you will need to prepare to discuss at the start of the meeting to set the scene:

- A brief description of what coaching is and how it works
- The overall benefits of using coaching as a way of developing an individual
- Your role as their coach
- The individual's role as performer
- Some ground rules about things such as confidentiality, taking notes, timing etc.
- Reasons why you have decided to coach them and why you have chosen them and not others (if this is the case)
- How long you expect the first meeting to take
- How long they can expect the overall coaching process to last

Getting it clear in your mind

Think about how you are going to explain all of the above before the meeting so that you come across confidently when you are explaining. If you are not able to easily and concisely explain what coaching is then your performer may already start to doubt your abilities and the process.

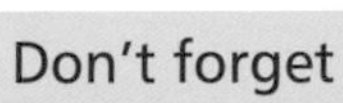

Practice how you are going to describe coaching for when you first raise the idea with your potential performer.

Before the first meeting

You may find you need to cover some of the above items before the first proper meeting. When you first approach an individual to suggest coaching and to set a date for the first meeting they are bound to have a number of questions at that time, especially relating to why you have decided to coach them.

Be prepared to give some explanation but don't get into too much detail at this stage – tell them that you will explain more in the coaching meeting itself.

Preparing questions

As we will see when we describe the coaching process in more detail, it is difficult to prepare very much in terms of specific questions.

It is important to remain very flexible in terms of the questions you ask. As with any conversation it is better to listen and react depending on the responses the performer gives.

Confidence with the process

Whilst you may not be able to prepare specific questions you should still begin by familiarizing yourself with the process so that you are confident with it and able to notice if the coaching is starting to go off track.

Make sure you are completely familiar with the coaching process before you start coaching.

Building rapport

Rapport can be described as an affinity, understanding or bonding between two people. In the coaching environment it is important that you and your performer (also sometimes referred to as the 'coachee') have a good rapport with each other and that you are able to talk together in a relaxed and informal way.

Building rapport before you get properly into the coaching session will ensure that, later in the meeting when you need to ask more searching questions, your performer feels comfortable and relaxed about responding openly and honestly. They may be reticent about responding if you ask sensitive questions too early in the meeting without having first built rapport.

Right from the start

To build rapport, start the meeting with some general conversation rather than launching straight into the coaching itself. Whilst you will need to be asking lots of questions throughout the coaching session, you should try to make your questions conversational rather than interrogatory in style.

Again, consider your relationship with the individual in other situations – do you already have a good rapport between you?

Summary

- Choose the venue for your coaching meeting carefully to provide the right environment – your office may seem the obvious choice but how will your performer react?
- Coaching off site can be a good idea to avoid distractions particularly if you use a hired meeting room
- Cafés can work well for less sensitive conversations and are an economical off-site option
- Avoid using restaurants for coaching as there are likely to be too many interruptions and distractions
- Body language plays a significant part in the process of communication so be mindful of the unspoken messages you send through your actions or choice of room layout
- If possible arrange the seating so that you are not facing each other and avoid having a desk between the two of you
- Book out more time in your diary than you estimate you will need in case the session overruns
- Take all necessary steps to ensure you manage any potential interruptions
- Plan what you are going to say in your introduction before the meeting and make sure you can explain coaching confidently
- Be prepared to answer some questions when you first introduce the idea of coaching to your performer and be able to explain why you have chosen to coach them over others
- Don't try and list out possible questions in advance of the meeting – you need to remain flexible to respond as needed
- Take a good look at your management style and, if necessary, make changes well before you decide to start coaching
- Spend time at the start of the meeting building rapport to relax yourself and your performer
- Avoid going straight into the coaching session with sensitive questions

4 The Coaching Process

We are now ready to look in detail at our process for conducting a coaching session. We will be following a simple, step-by-step process which takes you through each of the essential stages of a coaching meeting. As we describe each stage in turn we also provide suggestions of suitable questions to ask your performer.

44 It's as Easy as A-B-C...

46 A is for...

48 The Benefits of Aspirations

49 Asking for Aspirations

50 B is for...

51 Asking for Building Blocks

52 Listing Them All

53 Focusing on One

54 C is for...

56 Getting the Detail

58 D is for

60 More About Solutions

62 E is for...

64 Dealing with Blockages

65 The Next Meeting

66 F is for...

68 Summary

It's as Easy as A-B-C...

Having looked at what coaching is and how it can be used to enhance performance in the business context we will now look in more detail at how to actually conduct a coaching session.

Six steps to success

To help us we are going to use a simple process or model that will guide you through the coaching meeting a step at a time. The model we are going to use is a six-step process from A through to F where each of the steps represents a topic of conversation for you to have with your coachee.

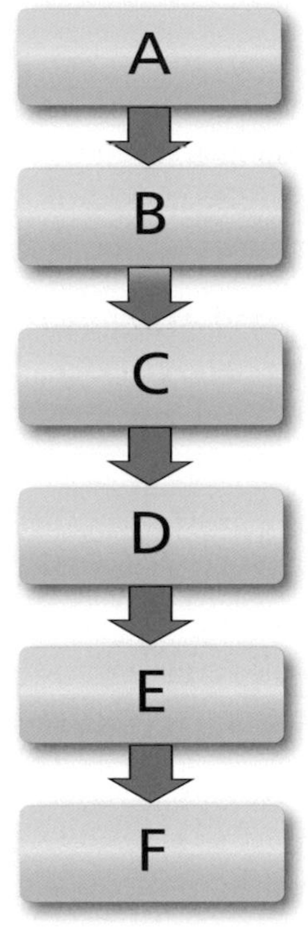

Keeping to the process

When we first describe the process and until you have become familiar with it, we suggest you keep fairly closely to the order as it is described. It is a well tried and tested process which works very effectively exactly as we describe it here – in sport and in business.

In the real world

As with any process, it is important to understand that the model is there to act as a guide and to keep you on track. In the real world we understand that it is not always possible or appropriate to stringently keep to the model regardless of the circumstances. This would be too rigid and may not ultimately result in the desired outcome.

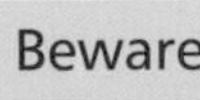
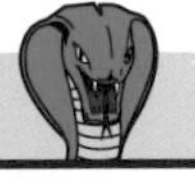

Beware

Straying from the model is fine if that is through choice but don't use this as an excuse for the fact you are really lost!

Coming off-track

There will be occasions, therefore, where it will be appropriate to allow the conversation to go a little off-track. Having a model enables you to see that it is off-track and choose how and when to bring the conversation back to the process.

There is a difference between consciously letting a meeting come away from a process because you calculate it is the best thing to do, and just allowing a meeting to drift with no structure or process in the first place.

Repeating stages

Whilst the model is linear in nature, moving from A through to B through to C and so on, you will come across occasions where you will need to repeat some stages or even loop back to an earlier stage in the process.

Ownership of the process

We have already stressed that the ownership of issues and the responsibility for decisions within coaching should rest with the performer. The only responsibility that you should take is for progressing the performer through the process.

Familiarity with the process

You therefore need to become very familiar with the process so that you can be flexible enough to know exactly where you are at any time and where you need to direct the conversation.

When you start using the model, you may find it helps to have the model noted down to remind yourself of the process and ensure you have remembered to cover each of the stages. It won't be long before you will feel completely familiar with each stage and can coach without any props to remind you.

Even your performer can learn it

As your performer becomes more familiar with the process you will find that they, too, will know whether the meeting is going in the right direction and can bring themselves back on track.

Practice first

Once you have finished reading this chapter, find opportunities to practice your skills and to familiarize yourself with the process well before deciding to coach for real with a member of your team.

You may want to try out some of your new coaching skills on your friends or, if you are learning to coach at the same time as a colleague, you could practice coaching each other.

Hot tip

Keep the model in front of you when you first start, to act as a reminder of each of the stages.

A is for...

Aspirations

Once you have built some rapport and introduced the coaching session to your coachee, the first topic to discuss is their ***Aspirations*** or long-term goals. During this first stage you need to encourage your coachee to think as far into the future as they can and then describe their long-term goals. Here are a few examples of aspirations:

- "I ultimately want to be running my own business"
- "I would like to become a junior/middle/senior manager"
- "I want to become a fully qualified accountant"
- "I want to become more relaxed about work with a clear work/life balance"
- "I want to become a confident presenter"
- "I want to be more assertive with my boss and peers"

You will see from the above list that the first three relate to ultimate career aspirations whereas the last three relate more to developing specific skills or behaviors.

If you have agreed to focus coaching on a particular topic or subject such as presenting, it is perfectly acceptable for the coachee to describe their aspiration in terms of their long-term goal, relating to just this area rather than for their whole career.

Hot tip

When we refer to the steps in our A-F model, we have used italics. Where we use a word, such as 'aspiration' in its generic form, it's written normally.

Finding the Aspirations

Who comes up with ***Aspirations***? These must, of course, come from your coachee. Only your coachee can know what their long-term goals are and the only way to find these out is to ask them.

This is the first opportunity to question your coachee and it is important you resist the urge to tell them what you think their aspirations should be.

A true Aspiration

If your coachee comes back with a response such as: "I want to become a confident presenter" it is not altogether clear whether their ultimate aspiration is to become a confident presenter. They may be describing a goal which would put them one step closer to a higher aspiration such as becoming a manager, where being a confident presenter would be a requirement.

Challenging your coachee

The best way to check this is simply to ask your coachee a question such as: "And what, ultimately, will you do once you are a confident presenter?" You may also want to test your coachee's commitment to their aspiration by asking: "How important is this aspiration to you?"

Don't judge

There is a difference between testing the validity or importance of you coachee's responses and you making a judgement over their aspiration – whether this is to encourage them to aim higher or to suggest they are more 'realistic'.

It is not your role to say, for instance: "Are you sure, because I think you are capable of much more than that?" or even worse: "I think you are going to have to be a bit more realistic about what you are hoping to achieve."

Beware

It is not your role to decide whether an aspiration is realistic or appropriate. Let your coachee discover this.

The Benefits of Aspirations

Sense of direction

Discussing *Aspirations* first is a logical start to the coaching process. But there is another reason for getting your performer to express their aspiration first. Once your performer is clear about their aspiration and feels motivated towards achieving it, it will provide a sense of direction and also give much more meaning to the rest of the coaching session. Effectively you have asked them to express a WIIFM – what's in it for them.

Hot tip

Reminding your coachee of their aspiration from time to time will help to keep them motivated.

Reminding the performer

From time to time, throughout the various coaching sessions, it is worth referring back to what your performer expressed as their aspiration. This enables you to check they haven't changed their aspiration and also reminds them why they are going through the coaching.

Even if your performer does not actually reach their stated aspiration – which of course may not be for several years – just having one helps to maintain their levels of motivation. If in a few weeks, months or even years, they decide it is not realistic then they will adjust it themselves.

As we shall see shortly, the realism of your performer's aspiration will become very apparent through later questioning and this may result in them lowering or even raising their sights.

Asking for Aspirations

Good questions

The quality of your questions makes a big difference to the effectiveness of your coaching. We are going to explore what makes a good question in the next chapter but for now here are a few examples of good questions you can ask to encourage your performer to think about their aspirations:

- What are your ultimate work aspirations or goals?
- What is important to you in terms of your long-term aspirations?
- Where, ultimately, in your work life do you want to get to?
- What are your long-term goals in relation to this issue?
- Within what timeframe do you hope to achieve this?

Don't forget 

Having asked a question about their aspirations, remain silent and allow your performer to think through their answer.

First response

When you ask these types of questions the first response you are likely to get is silence! You should normally treat this as a good thing because the question you have just asked is not necessarily an easy or straightforward one to answer.

We will look at this in more detail in the next chapter but if your performer doesn't immediately respond, don't jump in with another question to fill the silence. This will interrupt their thinking.

What do you think?

You may also find your performer throws the question back at you to ask for your opinion. Don't take this as permission for you to take control – push the question back to them again.

This reaction is often because the performer is not used to being asked for their opinions or views. As they become accustomed to taking more responsibility and responding to these types of questions, this will not happen as frequently.

B is for...

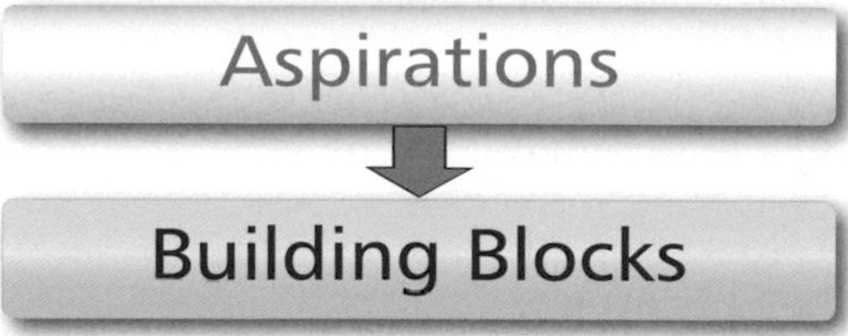

'B' stands for ***Building blocks*** and is the next stage in the coaching discussion. Having helped your coachee to establish their long-term goal, you now need to encourage them to break this down into more manageable 'chunks'.

Dreams into reality

A key aspect of coaching is that it helps a coachee to focus on the things that can make a difference. Many people have a vague idea of what they would like to do in the future but, for most, this will remain no more than just a fuzzy idea or a dream.

Don't forget 

One of the main reasons people don't ever achieve their dreams is because they never give any serious thought to how they might achieve them.

The reason most people don't ever achieve their aspirations or turn their dreams into reality is because they feel too big or far away. As a result, they don't do anything about achieving them.

Manageable chunks

By breaking their long-term A*spirations* into manageable sized goals, ***Building blocks,*** your coachee will be able to see more clearly their path to achieving their ultimate goal or goals. It converts what may have only ever felt like a dream into reality.

Finding the Building blocks

As with all the other parts of the model, the best way to get to the ***Building blocks*** is to ask your coachee.

Asking for Building Blocks

Good questions

To encourage your coachee to think through the possible ***Building blocks*** try asking questions such as:

- If you needed to break down your aspiration into bite-sized chunks, what would they be?
- What are the stepping stones you need to achieve to get you to your aspiration?
- What are the smaller goals you will need to achieve to get you to your goal?

Some examples

Taking one of the aspirations we listed on page 46: "I want to become a manager" let's look at what the ***Building blocks*** might be to achieve this:

- Become proficient at core management skills such as delegation, decision making, prioritization, leadership etc.
- Study and pass appropriate management qualifications
- Become fully proficient in the technical aspects of the role
- Become confident at presenting to small groups
- Become assertive when dealing with people at all levels
- Develop a good network of business connections

Breaking down Building blocks

If a ***Building block*** is too big and unmanageable then this in turn can be broken down into smaller sub-goals. So the ***Building block*** 'gaining core management skills' can be broken down into the individual skills and each of these can be broken down further if they still seem too big.

And what else?

This question is one of the most useful and easiest to ask and is used to encourage your coachee to come up with more ***Building blocks***. So, having come up with a ***Building block*** already, you can keep asking: "… and what else could you do?" or, "...and are there any other steps?" or "...and anything else?" and so on until they run out of possibilities.

Hot tip

If a *Building block* still seems too big to manage, get your coachee to break it down even further.

Listing Them All

Seeing the whole picture

If things are going well and your performer lists two or three ***Building blocks*** you may be tempted to stop at this point and move on. Depending on the aspiration, however, there may be many more ***Building blocks*** than this.

Without listing all of the ***Building blocks***, your performer won't be able to appreciate the full extent of what is needed to get to their aspiration. Seeing all the ***Building blocks*** is a first step towards them determining how realistic their aspiration really is.

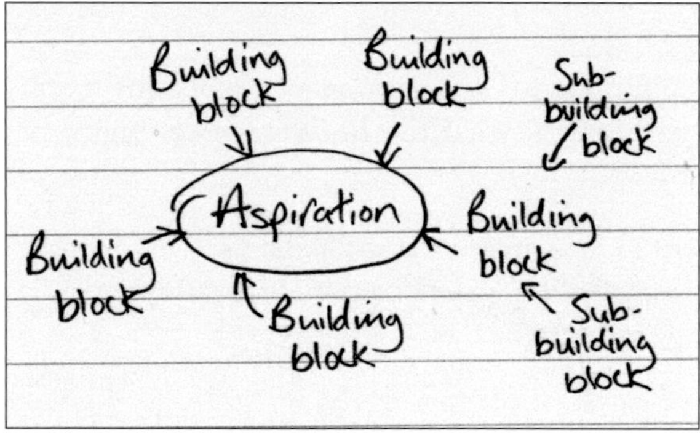

Beware

When asking for *Building blocks*, watch out that they are sub-goals to achieving their aspiration and not actions.

Goals not actions

If you take a look at our list of example ***Building blocks*** on page 51 you will see these are all written as goals or sub-goals:

- Become confident in...
- Study and pass...
- Become proficient in...

It is important that building blocks define the *achievement* of something towards the overall aspiration.

If, having asked for ***Building blocks***, you get a response such as: "I need more training" then you will need to re-phrase your question because 'training' is not a goal or sub-goal – it is an (unspecific) action or solution towards achieving a goal.

You could respond with a question such as: "What goal is this training going to help you to achieve?" The importance of this will become clearer as we move through the rest of the process.

Focusing on One

What's the priority?

Having listed all their ***Building blocks***, you then need to encourage your performer to decide which one (or possibly two) they are going to tackle first. Again, this is about encouraging your performer to focus on the things that will make a difference. There are a number of factors your performer can use to determine which ***Building block*** to tackle first:

- Tackle the easiest and get one under their belt quickly
- Do one of the enjoyable or more interesting ones to give a positive start
- Start with the most time-consuming because it may otherwise hold back others
- Start with the one which other ***Building blocks*** are dependent upon being completed first
- Do one which is topical – they may have the opportunity to practice it now
- Complete them in an order based on the progressive development of skills

Hot tip 

It will help your coachee to choose the first *Building block* they are going to work on if you list the factors they can use for determining its priority.

Let your performer decide

All of the above reasons are legitimate and it can help to describe these options to your performer so that they can then decide for themselves the basis on which they will determine the priority areas. It is important not to try to work on too many ***Building blocks*** at the same time otherwise, again, they may lose focus.

Interrelated Building blocks

Sometimes it can be helpful to tackle two ***Building blocks*** at the same time, particularly if they are in some way interrelated. An example would be ***Building blocks*** relating to questioning skills and listening skills. But be aware that tackling more than two ***Building blocks*** at a time will probably result in losing focus.

The remaining Building blocks

The reason for choosing one or two ***Building blocks*** is to keep your performer focused on developing the most important things first. You will not forget the other ***Building blocks*** because, as we will explain, you will need to revisit these again later in the process.

C is for...

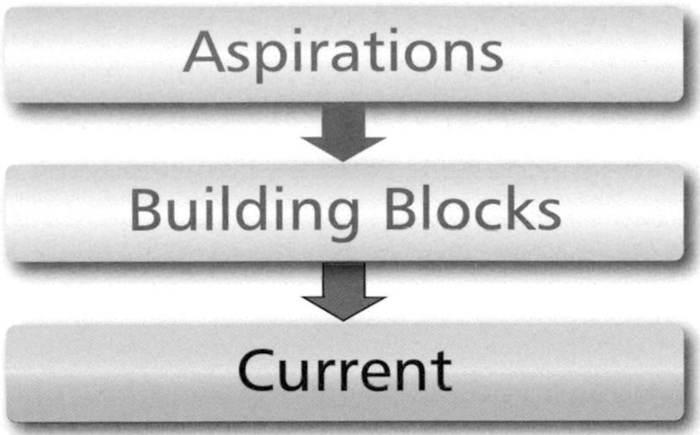

You are asking your coachee for their current capability in relation to their chosen *Building block* only.

'C' stands for ***Current*** – this is an assessment of where your coachee believes they are in terms of their current levels of knowledge, skills or experience relating to their chosen ***Building block.***

Once your coachee has a good understanding of their current level of ability they can compare it to where they need or desire to be. This, in turn, helps to define what is generally known as their 'development gap'.

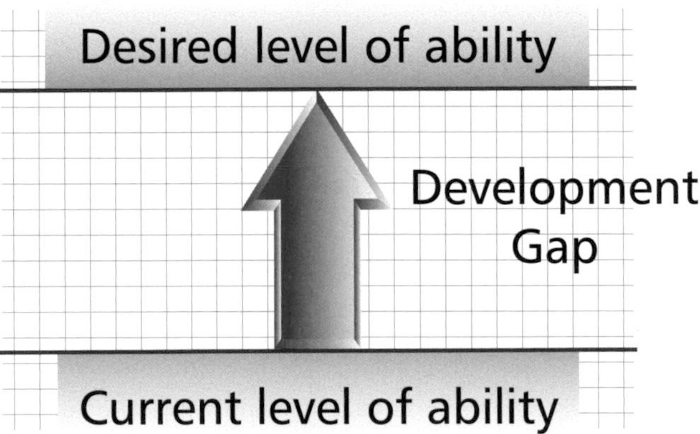

Generating self-awareness

As you should now start to realize, the best way to find this out is to ask your coachee. You may have your own views on your coachee's capability relating to their chosen ***Building block*** but you should resist giving them at this stage. By asking your coachee to make an assessment of their own position, you are encouraging them to become more self-aware.

Current relates to the chosen Building block

When you ask your coachee about *Current*, be very clear with them that this is in relation to a specific *Building block* and not an overall assessment of their general performance. Given that you need to keep your coachee focused, it is important you do not now let them stray back to a more general assessment of their overall performance.

Good questions

Here are some examples of questions you can use to encourage your coachee to think carefully about their *Current* state:

- In terms of your chosen *Building block*, how would you describe your current capability?
- For this first sub-goal you have chosen, how far off achieving it would you say you are?
- What would be your current assessment in terms of achieving this *Building block*? – both your strengths and weaknesses.
- How do you think others would assess you?

Go for detail

The more detail you can encourage your coachee to share, the more helpful this will be in terms of them truly getting to know themselves.

When you ask your coachee where they think they are in terms of a particular *Building block*, you may get a response such as: "Not too bad" or "I'm OK at that I think". This type of general response does not help them to really understand their true strengths and weaknesses in the chosen area and therefore will not help them to accurately define their development gap.

So, if you get such a response, it is an opportunity for you to add value by encouraging your coachee to be more focused in their thinking. You can try asking questions such as:

- When you say 'not so bad' exactly what do you mean by that?
- Can you describe what 'not so bad' looks like?
- When you say you are 'OK at that', where would you put OK on your scale of 1 to 10?

Hot tip 

The more detail you can encourage your coachee to give, the more valuable it is in terms of them getting to really understand the issue.

Getting the Detail

Hot tip

Using a scale of 1 to 10 is a good way to encourage your coachee to explain more about their *Current* state.

Scale of 1 to 10

Asking your coachee to use a scale of 1 to 10 is a really useful technique. Of course, whatever their response, it is not something that can be accurately measured. What your coachee means by a value they give such as 'six', may be very different to your impression of the same value.

Follow up

It is important that you don't comment on this value but follow up their response – whatever it is – with the question: "..so can you now describe what 'six' represents or means to you?"

This technique sometimes helps an individual to more accurately describe their ***Current*** state, particularly if they were having difficulty expressing themselves in the first place.

Compare with real examples

On occasions, you may feel that the coachee's own view is wildly inaccurate – either highly critical or, on the other hand, unrealistically positive! In either of these circumstances try to encourage your coachee to think through examples of how they have performed in real situations in order to better explore their capabilities.

It may be very tempting when listening to your coachee's responses to bring in your own assessment of their capability, especially if you do not agree with their own evaluation. Remember, though, that your coachee will believe what they say about themselves but won't necessarily believe your views. So try to resist adding your own opinions until they have finished.

Your opinion

Ultimately, you may want to bring in some of your own feedback based on your external viewpoint. This can be valuable but should only be done after your coachee has had an adequate opportunity to fully describe *Current* from their perspective.

Ask permission

If you do want to bring in some of your own comments it is best to ask permission to do this rather than manipulate your coachee into saying what you want them to say. You can ask permission simply by saying: "I have a couple of additional perspectives – would you mind if I throw these in?" Of course your coachee could say 'no' but this is very unlikely.

Providing feedback

When you do have your coachee's permission, ensure that your feedback relates specifically to the ***Building block*** being explored, focusses on their knowledge, skills and behaviors and is current – that is, not so old that it is irrelevant.

Backing it up

Any comments you make will have far more impact if you can back them up with examples or evidence. So rather than just saying: "You still appear to be finding it difficult to make decisions" you can add: "...for instance, last week when you needed to determine the best route for your project, I noticed your colleagues were having to push you to make a decision".

Balanced viewpoint

Finally, it is important that any feedback you give has a balance between positive and negative comments. It is easy to slip into providing only negative feedback.

Hot tip

It is always best to ask permission before providing any of your own feedback.

Don't forget

Provide a mix of positive and negative feedback and not just all positive or all negative.

D is for...

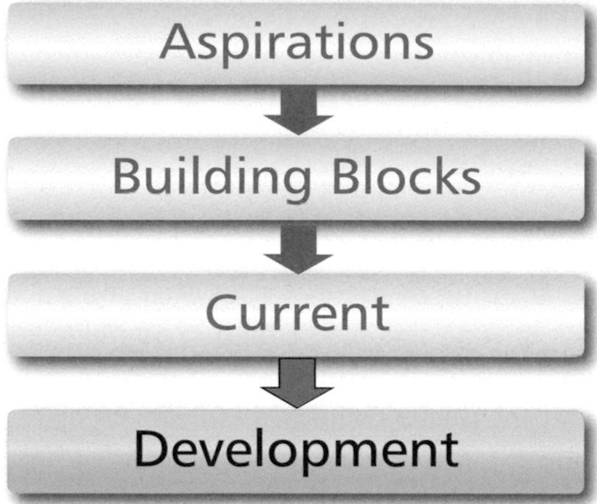

'D' represents *Development* – that is, what actions the performer could take in order to develop themselves to the level they need for their given *Building block*.

There may appear to be an obvious solution to completing the *Building block* such as going on a training course. One of the advantages of coaching, however, is solutions can be very specific and far more focused to the individual's need and learning style.

More is good

It is far better, at this stage, to encourage your performer to brainstorm as many possible solutions as they can. Again, don't be tempted to come in with your own ideas or judge those the individual comes up with themselves. The standard suggestions they are likely to come up with include solutions such as:

- Go on a training course or workshop
- Find out from a book or from the internet
- Learn on the job by trial and error

But there is a simple question which you can keep repeating and rephrasing which is: "…and what else could you do?" It is so simple, but if you keep asking this or similar questions, you will most likely encourage your performer to think of more ideas.

As with all brainstorming, you will find that the obvious answers always come out first and only then do you start to get the more interesting ones coming through.

Hot tip 

By repeating the question: "...and what else could you do?" you will encourage your coachee to come up with more ideas.

Here are some alternative development ideas your performer could consider:

- Read a specific management text on the subject
- Subscribe to a specialist journal or magazine
- Join a membership body
- Study towards professional qualifications
- Shadow a work colleague
- Take on a project using the required skills
- Role play with a friend or colleague
- Practice while recording with a camcorder
- Ask to take on additional responsibility

A more comprehensive list of possible development actions is provided in Chapter 10.

Make solutions specific

Some of the above solutions can be made much more specific and focused on a particular development area. I was once coaching an individual whose issue was that he needed to be able to listen carefully in meetings whilst also taking notes. He had realized that if he was listening intently he stopped taking notes and if he concentrated on taking notes he stopped listening!

Beware

Don't just let your coachee settle for the obvious development solutions - try to encourage different, more specific ideas.

This was a very specific issue and I am not aware of any courses or workshops on just this. His development suggestion was that, as he enjoyed watching sport on the television, he would practice by listening to sports commentaries whilst also taking notes.

His solution was ideal because he could practice his skills while doing something he enjoyed. It totally supported his ***Building block*** and, because he could record the program to play back later, he could also check how accurate he had been.

More About Solutions

Total solutions

One of the main reasons for encouraging your coachee to come up with a number of development suggestions is that they can then pick from these the most suitable to take forward.

Don't forget

Learning is broken down into knowledge skills and behaviors and the best combined solution will develop all three.

An ideal combination is to choose a range of solutions that provides some underpinning knowledge, then solutions to learn the required skills or behaviors and, finally, the opportunities to put these skills or behaviors into practice. So the total solution for, say, improving presentation skills may be:

- Watching a known expert to get some inspiration, then:
- Reading a book on presentation techniques, then:
- Practicing while recording, using a camcorder, and finally:
- Presenting for real

Learning styles

We all have our preferred ways of learning things and these are categorized into what are referred to as 'learning styles':

- People who prefer to just get stuck in and try things out – even if they end up making mistakes on the way
- People who like to watch and take copious notes and who like to explore the possibilities
- People who learn best by reading the theory first and thinking it through - putting it all in a logical order
- People who like to come up with new ideas, experiment and who hate getting bogged down in discussion

Hot tip

If you are interested in finding out more about learning styles there are many books and internet sites on the subject.

This is why you will find some people much prefer to read a book on a subject whilst others will say they would much prefer to go on a course to learn the same subject.

Knowing your coachee

You are unlikely to know your coachee well enough – particularly during the early meetings – to come up with development solutions based on styles of learning that will be just right for them. This is another good reason, therefore, not to try to impose your own development solutions on your coachee.

A quick exercise

Put on a jacket and, as you do so, note which arm you automatically put in first. Now take off the jacket and try putting it on again but this time put it on using your *other* arm first. For most people, forcing them to use the opposite arm first is enough to make it a very awkward and uncomfortable task.

You will note that just a small change such as swapping left to right or vice versa is often enough to make a task really difficult for someone.

If swapping left and right can make such a difference to the accomplishment of a simple task, imagine how the coach can complicate matters if they try to impose their own solutions on their coachee. This is yet another good reason for the coach to ask their coachee for their ideas rather than impose solutions.

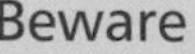

Beware

Avoid telling your coachee how to tackle their development gap as your suggestions may not be so easy for them to adopt.

Introducing your solutions

Having said what we have about the benefits of the coachee coming up with their own solutions, there may be a few occasions when your coachee runs out of ideas and you need to introduce one or two of your own suggestions. In this situation, just as we described under *Current*, you should ask permission before bringing your suggestions into the discussion.

Which to commit to

Hopefully at this stage in the coaching process your coachee has a long list of possible development actions to develop their chosen *Building block*. The final part of this stage is for your coachee to decide which of those development ideas they are going to commit to.

Not all their initial suggestions will necessarily be practical and some may be similar versions of the same action. Your coachee can decide the best combination to provide a total solution.

E is for...

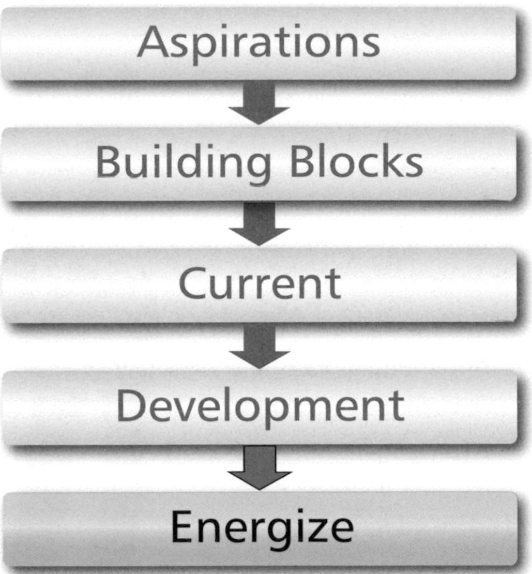

Many coaches, having assisted an individual in determining a number of development solutions, will send their performer on their way in the belief that they have done their job and the performer will now put these actions into place. Regrettably this is not always the case and why we now need to look at how to *Energize* the performer.

Energizing your coachee is a critical step to ensure the best chance of success and should not be left out.

The most crucial step

This last step is probably the most crucial of all the steps and without it there is every chance that nothing will happen after the meeting and thus the first coaching session will all have been a waste of time.

Motivating your performer

To *Energize* we create the right levels of motivation to ensure that your performer feels fully committed and empowered to work at their development actions. *Energizing* breaks down into three important elements:

- Firming up on development actions
- Ensuring your performer is motivated to complete them
- Managing any blockages to them succeeding

On the next page we are going to look at each of these in turn.

Firming up the actions

When your performer initially suggests possible development actions this may be merely a list of ideas. Once they commit to particular actions, you can encourage your performer to think in more detail about how they will actually make these happen.

So if your performer says they intend to 'practice', what do they actually plan to do? This response is far too vague at this stage. Challenge their response by asking questions such as:

- Who will they practice with and how often?
- What materials or resources will they need?
- How will they know they are practicing the right things?

Ensuring they are motivated

For this you can use the 1-10 scale: "On a scale of one to ten, how motivated are you about taking on this action?" If they respond with a low value then ask: "So what can you do to make it more like a nine or ten?" Leave your performer feeling motivated and looking forward to completing their development.

Hot tip 

Find out how motivated your performer is about their development plans by using a scale of one to ten.

Managing the blockages

Blockages are the factors or problems that could get in the way of your performer completing their development plans – these should not to be confused with ***Building blocks***. Through questioning, encourage your performer to highlight as many blockages as they can that they foresee could get in the way of them completing their actions.

Dealing with Blockages

Types of blockages

Blockages fall into two types: 'Self blockages' are ones normally relating to the individual's mindset or levels of motivation which are likely to put them off fulfilling an action – often referred to as 'mental blocks'. Examples of self-blockages include:

- I won't be able to do that
- What if I fail?
- I'm not very good at studying

'World blockages' are external factors that could impact their chances of success. Here are a few examples:

- I have too much work to do
- Home life makes it difficult to concentrate on study
- I can't think of any opportunities to practice
- There are no suitable projects to take on

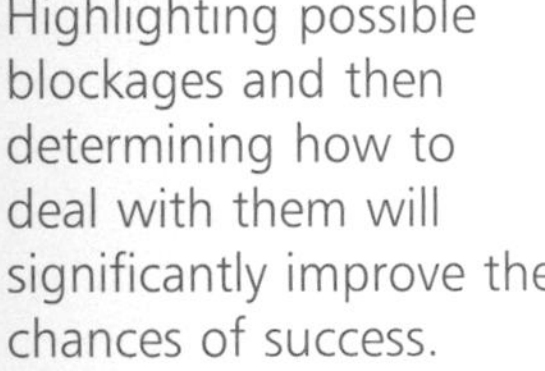

Highlighting possible blockages and then determining how to deal with them will significantly improve the chances of success.

Pre-empting the blockages

Any of the blockages on your performer's list could delay or stop them from completing their actions. So once your performer has highlighted all possible blockages, ask them to consider, for each one, what actions they will take to deal with it should it occur. Clearly they will not be able to foresee every possible problem but it is surprising how many can be planned for. Armed with a list of solutions for tackling their blockages, if any do occur, your performer will know how to handle them.

The Next Meeting

Agree timescales

Your performer should now have a set of well-defined actions that they are fully committed to completing. All that remains is for them to determine how long they expect to take to complete each action and when you will next meet to review their progress.

Your next meeting

The timing for your next meeting should be determined by your performer. As a guide, if the length of time between sessions is too short your performer will not have had enough time to do anything about completing their actions. They will also start to get frustrated because there may be only a slight improvement since the last meeting.

On the other hand, if the period in between is too long, there is a danger they will let it drift, thinking they have plenty of time to complete their actions. Typically you should aim to agree a timescale between meetings of between two and six weeks.

Diarize it

Get an actual date and time in your calendars and then make sure you stick to it. If you just agree to meet at some point in the future without picking an actual date and time, inevitably it will drift and your performer is likely to be less driven to completing their actions.

Mid-review

You do not have to wait until the performer has completed an action before meeting again. If they are reading a book which is going to take a couple of months or more, it may be worth meeting at least once in between. You can still review what they have learned so far and what other actions they have been working on.

Beware

Leaving too long between coaching sessions will result in the development actions drifting.

F is for...

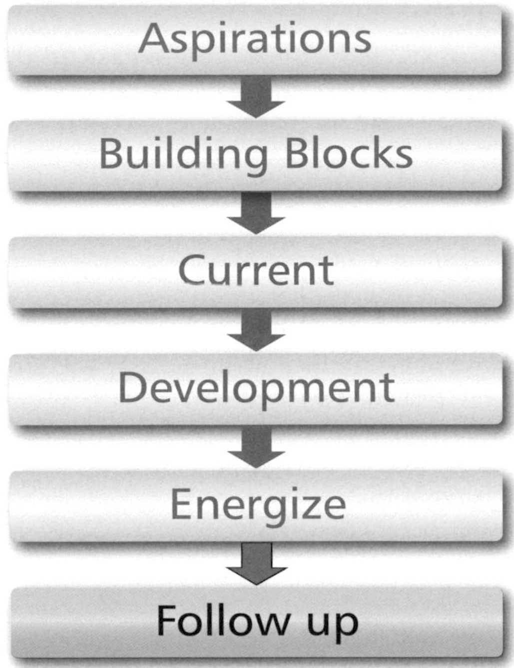

The last stage in the process, 'F' is for ***Follow up***. In fact, this is the first of what is likely to be a number of follow-up meetings.

Responsibility for progress

When you meet again with your coachee, if they have been taking responsibility for their development and are 'on receive', they will be keen to feedback progress to you. They will want to tell you what has worked and what has not been so successful.

Good questions to ask

If you need to encourage your coachee to give you feedback or need them to expand on their experiences to give both their positive and negative findings, you can try some of the following questions:

- How have you got on with your development actions?
- What has worked/has not worked?
- What have you learned from taking on these actions?
- Where are you now, on your scale of 1-10 in terms of completing this ***Building block***?

Hot tip

Encourage your coachee to self-appraise how they got on. If they are 'on-receive' they will be keen to tell you what has happened since you last met.

Go for detail

Just as we described under ***Current***, when you ask your coachee how they have progressed, they may give you a very unspecific answer such as: "Not bad really" or hopefully even "Great!" It is important that you encourage your coachee to be more specific in their description – not so that you get to know more about their experience but so that they are encouraged to analyze their own experiences in more detail.

The good and not so good

Depending on the type of individual you are coaching, you may find they emphasize either the good or bad experiences. More pessimistic people are likely to dwell on problems they experienced whilst the more optimistic or confident will tell you how good it all was. In reality, it is likely some activities will have worked whilst others will have been less successful. Encourage your coachee to give a balanced appraisal of their experience.

Celebrate the small successes

Because you are likely to be meeting up every few weeks, there is a danger that small improvements will go unnoticed. As coach, you may be in a better position to recognize improvements, however small they are, since the last time you met. Look out for those little changes and highlight them to your performer.

Don't forget

Your coachee may not notice slight improvements. Look out for opportunities to recognize and celebrate success.

Reviewing next steps

Once your coachee has discussed with you their progress towards completing their development actions there are a number of possible next steps. We are going to examine these in more detail in Chapter 7.

Summary

We have covered a lot of ground in this chapter describing each stage of the coaching model in turn. Here are some of the key points from each part of the process:

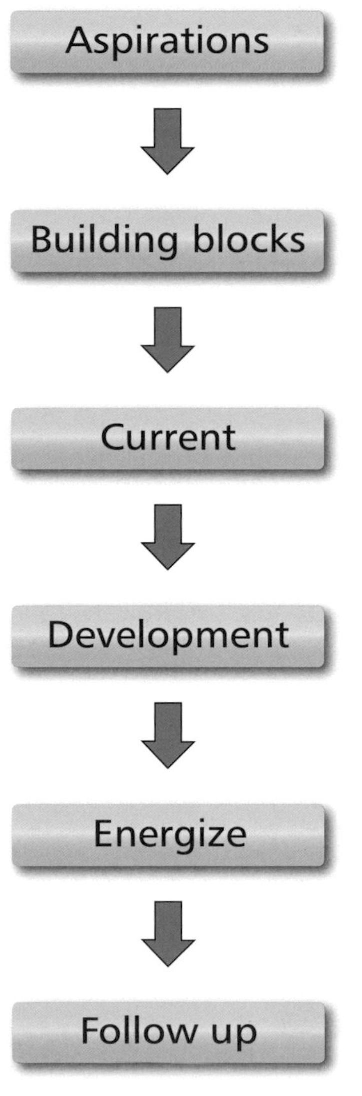

Build rapport with your coachee before encouraging them to think as long term as possible and describe their career and life *Aspirations*.

Your coachee needs to break down their aspiration into manageable sized *Building blocks*. They can then decide which they will tackle first.

By encouraging them to assess themselves your coachee should describe in detail their *Current* state and so understand their development gap.

Encourage your coachee to come up with as many different *Development* solutions as possible, matching their learning style to create a total solution.

Energizing is in three parts: Firming up the actions, ensuring they have the motivation and managing any potential blockages.

The *Follow up* meetings allow your coachee to describe what has worked and what they have learned from completing their development actions.

Use this page as a reminder of the main stages, particularly when practicing. We will revisit it later in the book to explore how to progress the coaching as they complete their *Building blocks*.

5 Supporting Skills

We have spent a lot of time so far looking at the coaching process. In this chapter we look at some of the key supporting skills and behaviors which will ensure your coaching sessions are truly effective. Most important of all the coaching skills are questioning and listening. All of the skills we cover are also highly relevant to many other management situations.

70 Questioning
71 Open and Closed Questions
72 High-gain Questions
74 Keeping it Conversational
75 Leading Questions
76 Questioning to Focus
78 More on Questioning
79 Listening
80 Body Language
82 Barriers to Listening
83 Active Listening
84 Reflecting
85 Summarizing Examples
86 Taking Notes
88 Mind Mapping
90 Summary

Questioning

You ask questions every day as part of your normal conversations with people – friends, business colleagues as well as strangers. You probably haven't previously given much thought to the questions you ask, their construction or effectiveness.

But by now you will have probably realized that in the context of coaching, the quality of your questioning is one of the most critical skills for you to focus on. Of course, as well as questioning your performer, you also need to concentrate on listening to their answers!

Reasons for asking questions

In a business context you may be used to asking questions – normally for your benefit, to find out information. For example:

- To ask a member of your team how they are progressing with a piece of work
- In a selection interview, to test a candidate's level of knowledge and their level of experience
- During a performance appraisal, to find out how a member of your team thinks they have been performing

In coaching, our reasons for questioning are quite different. There are three primary reasons for asking questions. They are to encourage your performer to:

1. Think through issues themselves and so raise their levels of awareness
2. Take personal responsibility for their own development
3. Focus on the things that are going to make a difference

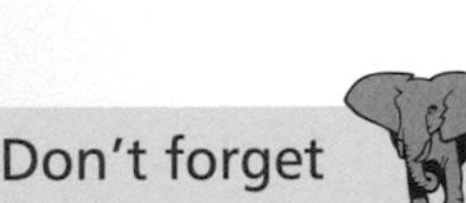

Don't forget

When using questions as a coach you are encouraging your coachee to think through issues rather than trying to find out information for your benefit.

Asking questions which are for the benefit of your performer and not for you requires a very different mindset and will affect the types of questions you will need to ask. With this in mind we are going to describe a number of useful questioning techniques to use when coaching.

Open and Closed Questions

We will start off with some important foundations. Firstly, all questions can be described as being either 'open' or 'closed'.

Closed questions

The generally accepted definition of a closed question is one which can be answered with either a 'yes' or a 'no'.

You will be well practiced with using closed questions if you have ever played the game 'twenty questions'. They start with words such as: 'is', 'was', 'does', 'have', 'can' and 'should'. Try asking someone a closed question and see what response you get. Because they only have to decide 'yes' or 'no' you should find that the person you ask is able to respond quite quickly.

Hot tip

Open questions start with a 'W' (other than 'how') and will lead to more than just a 'yes' or 'no' answer.

Open questions

Broadly, all open questions can be categorized as questions which result in a response other than just a 'yes' or 'no'. They are very easy to recognize in that they generally start with a 'W' – They are: 'when', 'where', 'who', 'which', 'why' and the only one not to start with a 'W' is 'how'.

For most situations you will find you are far more effective if you always try to ask open questions. You will find you get to the point far quicker than having to use a series of closed questions. It is also less likely you will lead your performer into coming up with answers you think they should arrive at.

High-gain Questions

Although open questions are generally considered more effective than closed questions it is still possible to ask open questions that will result in just one-word answers.

"What color is that car?" for example, is only likely to result in the simple answer: "Red", for example. This may be slightly better than the response from a closed question but we need to use questions which will result in far more information than just a one-word answer.

Lots of information

To be an effective coach you need to ask questions that will draw out a lot of information in one go and encourage your coachee to open up their thoughts. For this we use 'high-gain' questions. These are a type of open question that encourage your coachee to give responses that are:

- Future oriented
- Opinion-based
- Much more than just one-word answers

Hot tip 

High-gain questions are especially useful for exploring your coachee's *Aspirations*.

Good high-gain questions

As a form of open question, high-gain questions still start with 'what', 'where', 'when', 'who', 'which' and 'how'. Here are some examples of high-gain questions. You will see that they are especially useful when exploring *Aspirations*:

- Where do you see your career going over the next five to ten years?
- What are your long-term goals?
- What things are important to you in your work life?
- What makes you feel that?
- How do you think you are going to achieve that?

Give some thought

High-gain questions are not that easy to come up with on the spur of the moment. Whilst you cannot prepare specific questions in advance of your meetings, it is worthwhile thinking through some high-gain questions so you can become familiar using them.

Don't fill the silence

When you ask a good high-gain question your performer is likely to need some time to think through their response. Remember you are asking them to think into the future or about their opinions. As a result, they may need time to consider their response and may not therefore instantly reply.

Beware

Don't be tempted to fill the silence after a high-gain question with closed questions.

You may be tempted, if they don't respond immediately, to fill the silence by re-wording the same question or by asking a series of closed questions which will be easier for your performer to respond to. Filling the silence will destroy the impact of your high-gain question and break your coachee's train of thought. Here's what could happen:

Coach: "What's important to you in terms of your work life at the moment?" (A good high-gain question to do with aspirations)

Coachee: Silence (Because they are thinking)

Coach: "For instance, are you looking for ways of taking more responsibility?" (Closed and leading question to fill the silence)

Coachee: "Urm" (Still trying to think but now also having to think and respond to the closed question as well)

Coach: "...or are you happy at the level you are?" (Now the coach is starting to play twenty questions!)

As you will hopefully appreciate, these closed questions spoil what could have been a valuable first high-gain question.

TV chat show hosts

When a chat show host asks a guest a question about their career they will often ask high-gain questions such as: "So what are your future plans for your career?" Notice, though, that they will often follow it up with a string of closed questions.

This is acceptable for television where silence is not something which is desired but it is not what we are looking for when coaching.

Keeping it Conversational

It is important to keep the coaching session relaxed and conversational. Even though you may be asking a lot of questions, at no time should the meeting become an interrogation. You otherwise risk your coachee becoming defensive and therefore less open and engaged.

Assumptive questions

By keeping your questions relaxed and conversational you will find even some closed questions can be phrased to encourage more than a 'yes' or a 'no'.

One form of these is known as 'assumptive questions'. These are questions where we make an assumption and check it with the other person – normally using a closed question. We use these quite naturally in our everyday conversations. Here is an example:

Hot tip

Your coachee will open up far more if you keep your questioning conversational.

"Aren't you planning on going on holiday in the summer?"

Based on our definition of a closed question this ought to elicit a response of either 'yes' or 'no'. But as part of a relaxed conversation very few people would respond so abruptly. In reality they will either confirm that they are going on holiday or correct your assumption with some explanation as to why they aren't going on holiday.

Good assumptive questions

Here are a couple of examples of assumptive questions used in a coaching context:

- "You appear to me to come across as quite confident in those situations, is that right?"
- "Didn't you say you were thinking of starting a home study course later this year?"

Caution

It is important that, in making assumptive questions, you do not in any way lead your coachee – leading questions are not helpful in coaching.

Leading Questions

Before exploring more about questioning we need to warn against the use of leading questions. Remember, your prime concern is encouraging your coachee to come up with their own views and ideas. Your views are of much less importance.

When, from time to time you have ideas, it can be very tempting to want to 'help' your coachee by giving them your advice or guidance. This, as we have discussed, would be taking back responsibility from your coachee.

Avoid manipulation

You may think that you can bring in your ideas by encouraging your coachee to 'come up with the idea themselves' through the use of leading questions. But leading questions can come across as very manipulative and will encourage your coachee to start trying to second guess what you are wanting them to answer. This is arguably worse than just suggesting the idea yourself in the first place. Here are a couple of examples of leading questions:

"If you were to aim higher and get to a more senior role, that would be great wouldn't it?" This is clearly steering the coachee to think again about their response, persuading them to aim higher.

"Don't you want to be the top sales person and earn lots of additional commission?" Not only does this lead the coachee into having to aim to be the best sales person but it also makes the assumption that the individual's prime motivation is money.

Break the habit

It is very easy to slip into leading questions and if this is something you find yourself doing naturally, you may need to work hard to break the habit.

Beware 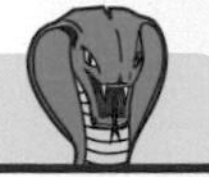

You should avoid, at all times, the use of leading questions that encourage your coachee to say what you are thinking.

Questioning to Focus

We have previously highlighted that coaching can be a very effective way of helping individuals to become more focused in their thinking. Through carefully structured questioning you can gradually focus the thoughts of your performer from vague ideas into concrete plans and activity.

Focus via the coaching process

The structure of the coaching process itself is designed to channel your performer's thinking towards a focused set of actions. Starting from their high-level ***Aspiration*** you channel your performer's thoughts towards more manageable ***Building blocks*** and then to the specific ***Building block*** that they decide to work with first.

The focus is then applied to this one ***Building block*** to determine the specific actions which will become part of their clearly defined set of actions.

Convergence

There will also be opportunities *within* each stage of the coaching process for you to gradually focus your performer's thinking. This is especially important when getting your performer to define their ***Aspirations*** and also later in the meeting when you are encouraging them to firm up on their development actions.

Where your performer is struggling to get clarity in their thinking or where you hear them using vague or 'fuzzy' language in response to a question, you can test and challenge this through further questioning to help them to have real clarity over their thinking. This is shown in the diagram below:

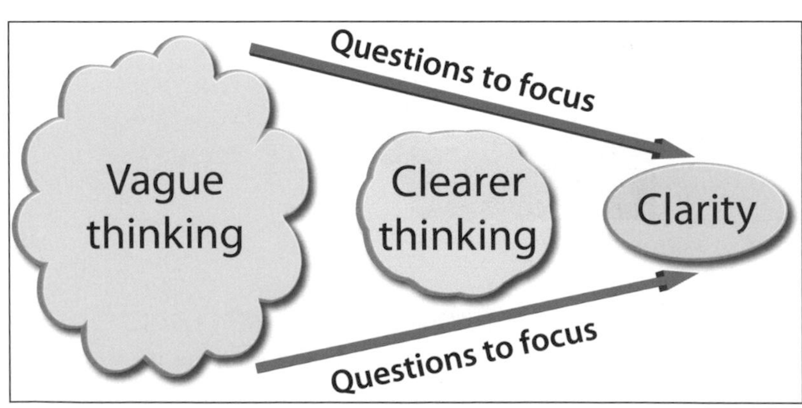

Good questions

Here are some examples of questions you can use to help your performer focus:

- When you say you're "not very good at this", what exactly do you mean?
- How can you make that more specific?
- How important is that to you?

Chipping away the unwanted

There is a children's joke which asks how you make a statue of an elephant – the answer is you chip away the bits that don't look like an elephant. If your performer cannot get clarity over what they want directly, it can sometimes be more useful to suggest they chip away the bits that they definitely don't want so that they can see what they are left with.

Divergence

There will be other times when it can benefit your performer to consider a number of ideas before focusing on the one or two they decide to take forward. This can be a useful technique where your performer is following one traditional or obvious route without considering any other options first.

Encourage your performer to brainstorm all the possibilities first – watch that you don't take over. It may help to write all of the ideas on a flip chart or whiteboard. When they have come up with a number of options you can then question your performer to focus them back down to just one or two preferred options.

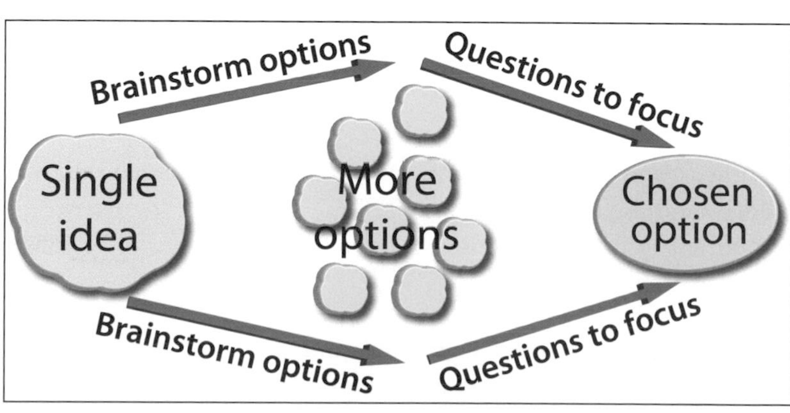

More on Questioning

Probing

In our normal lives we ask many questions as part of general conversation but will normally take responses at face value. In coaching you can add great value by questioning to a much deeper level and so, again, encourage your coachee to think more deeply about what they have just said.

Hot tip

If your coachee uses vague language, question them to help them understand better what they really mean.

So when your coachee gives you a response such as: "I've always had a thing about going to interviews" what exactly do they mean by 'a thing' and is it really 'always' and what type of interviews are they referring to?

Listen out for vague language and ask your coachee to clarify more precisely what they mean. By probing in this way you are helping your coachee to be more focused in their thinking.

The question 'why?'

Of all the open questions we described earlier, the only ones you should try to avoid using in coaching are those starting with the word 'why?' Questions starting with 'why' are open questions but invariably result in the coachee having to reply with a justification. For example: "Why do you get nervous over making presentations?"

why?
why?
why?
why?

There are alternative, softer, ways of phrasing this same question to make it sound less abrupt. You can rephrase it to: "What is it that makes you nervous when making presentations?"

Tell me

Another technique you can use, provided your style is relaxed, is a command used as a question: "Tell me about your long-term aspirations" or "Tell me more about your own assessment of your current capabilities."

Neither of these are strictly questions but should encourage a similar response to a high-gain question.

Listening

Listening skills

Having explored some of the many skills and techniques for asking questions, we now need to consider how to truly listen to what is said by your coachee when they respond.

There is an old adage which says that we all have two ears and one mouth and we should use them in this proportion. This is certainly the case for coaching where you need to do a lot more listening than talking.

A single, well thought through question can result in your coachee responding for some time with little further interjection from you. You then just need to listen – carefully and accurately.

Reasons for listening

As with questioning, you are not listening in order to gather information for your benefit. You should be listening in order to:

- Note key points which you can summarize for your coachee to help them maintain focus and clarity
- Pick up on any unfocused statements and then encourage more clarity (for the benefit of your coachee)
- Note the way your coachee responds and so determine any underlying issues through further questioning
- Keep a note of where you both are in the process and so ensure you stay on track

Body Language

Body language is a very important part of the listening process and it is therefore something that needs to be considered whilst we are focusing on listening skills.

When you next find yourself listening to someone as part of a normal conversation, make a note of your actions and responses. Most likely you will find that you nod from time to time, probably making some eye contact with the other person as well as making noises such as: 'uh-huh' , 'yes' or 'mm'.

Signals of encouragement

These are all forms of body language or non-verbal communication which signal to the other person that you are listening to them and that you are interested. The person talking may not consciously notice you doing this but if you were to force yourself to stop doing these actions it would probably feel very unnatural and uncomfortable for both of you. You may also notice that the other person finds it more difficult to keep going and ultimately shuts up.

Encourage your coachee to talk; use body language signals to show that you are interested and engaged.

Keeping them talking

So if, on the other hand, you do a little more nodding and use 'yes' or 'uh-huh' more (but not too much) to show your interest, you will find that your gestures encourage your performer to keep speaking. Your body language demonstrates that you are listening and therefore encourages them to continue.

Eye contact

This is another important element of non-verbal communication. Eye contact is generally good as it shows that you are listening and attentive. If you look down or away from your performer you may come across as rude or disinterested.

Even when taking notes, if you need to look down to write, try to ensure you make eye contact from time to time. Do watch, though, that your eye contact doesn't turn into a stare. This can be off-putting and possibly scary! You can make eye contact less intimidating by looking sometimes at their one eye, then the other, to their mouth and sometimes to your notes.

Hot tip

Good levels of eye contact show that you are interested but watch it doesn't become a stare.

Lean forward

The way you sit also signals to your performer your level of attentiveness. If you sit back in your chair you may look more relaxed but, again, may appear as if you are disinterested. If, on the other hand, you lean slightly forward towards the front of your seat you will look more alert and engaged.

Provide facial feedback

Above all, try to ensure that you animate your facial expression. Watch that you don't concentrate so hard that your face seizes up into a stare. You should be naturally moving your head, smiling, frowning, moving your eyebrows and making facial expressions in response to what your performer is telling you.

Make it genuine

Whilst we have provided some hints and tips on how to encourage your performer through your body language, it is important that you don't overdo any of these techniques and that, above all, you appear sincere. Before making any changes, focus on how you generally react as a listener and, if you find that you need to, try bringing in just one or two of these techniques.

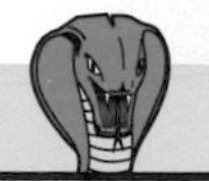

Beware

Watch that you don't overdo your body language otherwise it may not come across as sincere.

Negative signals

It is very easy to inadvertently – and sometimes falsely – send out signals that you are bored or disinterested. Try to avoid:

- Yawning
- Fiddling with or clicking your pen
- Looking at your watch

Barriers to Listening

When we listen to people during everyday conversation we only pick up a small fraction of what is actually being communicated. Particularly when you first start coaching you may be more concerned about what question you are going to ask next instead of listening to the response to your last question.

It is also very difficult to maintain 100% concentration when someone is talking – particularly over a long period of time. There is always the danger your attention will drift and your inner thoughts will start to distract you. If you don't listen carefully you may miss some of the real detail and meaning behind what is being said.

We filter

We all unconsciously 'filter' so that we only hear what we want to hear. This is why two people can listen to the same message but come away with two different interpretations. It is therefore critical in coaching to listen without filtering what you hear.

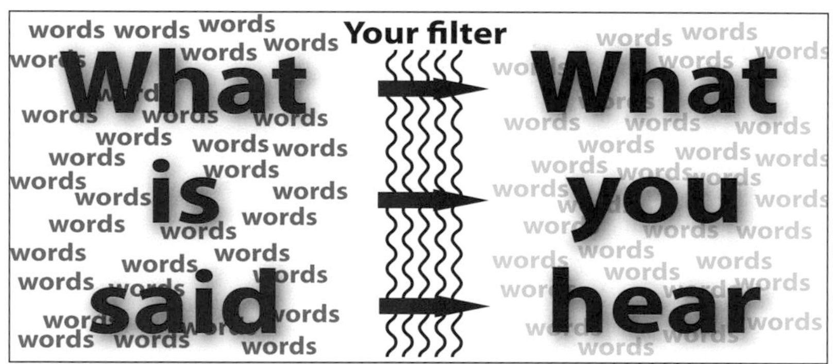

Hot tip

Pay attention to your coachee's body language as well as your own. Notice if their words don't match their mannerisms.

Coachee's body language

As well as being aware of the effect of your own non-verbal signals you need to pay attention to those being transmitted by your coachee. Until now you may not have had much concern over the signals and messages that are being subtly conveyed through the other person's body language but in coaching you need to be attentive to this to be truly effective.

Notice, for instance, if their body language agrees with what they are saying. If they say: "I'm really committed to making this work" but their facial expression does not look so committed, you may want to probe further to understand their true feelings.

Active Listening

This is a technique that goes much further than normal listening and is one that can help you to concentrate and remember what your coachee is saying.

To actively listen, in addition to nodding and making noises to indicate your interest, at appropriate stages when your coachee has finished making key points you need to provide a brief summary by paraphrasing what they have just said.

Active listening works for a number of reasons:

- To summarize accurately you will have to listen and concentrate that much more
- To paraphrase rather than just repeat their words, your brain has to compute what has been said to change the wording slightly – this helps you to remember what has been said
- When you summarize you are encouraging your coachee by proving you have heard what they are saying
- If your summary doesn't accurately reflect what your coachee meant they are then able to correct your understanding
- Summarizing helps your coachee to remain focused

Don't change the meaning

When paraphrasing it is important that you don't change or twist their original meaning or add your own viewpoint. Your summary should be as close as possible to your coachee's original meaning.

Check

Having summarized, you can finish with a closed question such as: "Does that sound right?" or "Have I got that right?" This will reassure your coachee and also gives them the opportunity to confirm or, alternatively, correct your summary and clarify what they meant.

Beware

It is important when paraphrasing that you accurately reflect what your coachee has said and don't change its meaning.

Reflecting

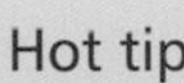

Hot tip

It can be very powerful to replay the precise words your coachee uses, particularly when it is a distinctive phrase.

Using their words

For most summaries, as we have described, it is best to paraphrase what your performer has said. This will ensure your summaries are kept short and to the point. There are some occasions, however, where it can be particularly powerful to replay or reflect back to your performer the actual words they used.

For example, your performer may use distinctive words to describe their future aspiration: "I would really like to get to a level of confidence so that, when I am making a presentation, I do not just turn to jelly."

Be sure to note the expression "turn to jelly" and then you can quote it exactly as they said it in your summary. This will remind them of their aspiration far more vividly than if you just paraphrase it.

Don't overdo it

Whilst this is a very useful and powerful technique, you should avoid using it too often. If you do, it will make your active listening summaries too long and some of its impact will be lost. Use it just to emphasise your performer's key points and where they use distinctive expressions.

Key stages

As well as paraphrasing as part of active listening, it is often very helpful to provide a summary at the end of each of the key stages in the coaching process. This will ensure that you both keep on track and it will also help your performer to remain focused.

Examples

On the next page we have provided example summaries for each of the key stages in the coaching process based on a first coaching session with an inexperienced first line manager. The words in inverted commas reflect the actual words the performer used.

Summarizing Examples

A "You said that ultimately, your aspiration is to become a senior manager of a medium sized team involved in some aspect of customer service. This, you felt would give you the right level of 'responsibility and challenge' – both of which are things you said are important to you."

B "You listed a number of ***Building blocks*** which, if you achieve them, will get you to your aspiration. As you were talking I noted down the following [description of each ***Building block***]– do these sound about right? Of these, you felt that the one you wanted to work on first was 'becoming better at delegation' which you chose because it was something you would have the opportunity to practice now."

C "When I questioned you about your current delegation skills you initially said you 'weren't very good' at this. When I asked you to expand on this you said that you could do it but you said you sometimes felt very 'awkward' about delegating because you know everyone is already very busy and also that these are people you worked alongside before being promoted."

D "Given what the real issue is, you decided that you wanted to focus on how to become more comfortable about delegating and also look at how to determine who to best delegate to. You came up with a number of development ideas which included [list the development actions] three of which were ones you felt you wanted to pursue."

E "You felt really committed to all three actions and wanted to start straight away. One of your suggestions was to keep a list of who you delegated to and what work you delegated. You scored yourself 6/10 in terms of your level of motivation because you felt you might not get to do it until next week. You thought the best way to make it happen was to put a note in your electronic diary. Finally, you suggested we meet again three weeks from now."

Taking Notes

Taking notes is an essential element of coaching. Most coaching sessions are likely to be quite involved and you will, at the very least, need to record the main decisions, ideas and key phrases your coachee comes up with. They need to be comprehensive enough to refer back to when you are summarizing during the meeting but also at subsequent meetings.

However, your attention needs to be focused on your coachee as much as possible and if you get too bogged down in lengthy note taking you will not be able to give them your full attention.

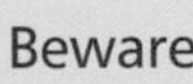

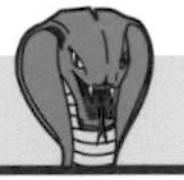

Beware

Watch that your note taking doesn't spoil the flow of the coaching session. Just note the key points.

Eye contact

Another reason for not taking too many notes is that while you are looking down to write your notes you are not able to maintain sufficient eye contact with your coachee.

Keeping the flow

You should definitely not slow down or interrupt the flow of your coachee's responses just because you can't keep up with your notes. If you are a slow writer, at least make sure you note the key themes and also any specific phrases your coachee uses.

Ultimately, the level and style of note-taking is your personal choice provided you can recall parts of the meeting as and when you need to.

Key stages

There are certain critical decisions you need to record and these relate to each of the key stages in the coaching process. It will certainly be useful to record your coachee's aspiration once this has become clear in their mind. Remember that you will want to refer to this from time to time – not just in the first meeting but also in follow-up meetings to remind your coachee why they are being coached.

Noting Building blocks

It is worth noting your coachee's ***Building blocks*** as they think of them. Hopefully your coachee will come up with a number of ***Building blocks*** but these may not come out in any particular order. Unless your coachee is taking notes it will be up to you to keep a track of what they have listed. You can summarize these to keep them fresh in your performer's mind.

Handing over responsibility

When it comes to recording development actions and the details which will come from ***Energizing***, it is better for your coachee to record these themselves. There are two good reasons for handing this over to your coachee:

- It will encourage them to take ownership of their action plan
- If they find it hard to read your writing they may not be able to work out what they planned to do

Hot tip

Give the responsibility for recording the development actions to your coachee. This ensures they take ownership of them.

Action log

In Chapter 10 we have provided a sample action log which you can replicate and use with your coachee and get them to complete. Your coachee should take this away with them to remind them of their actions. It is up to you whether you want to keep a copy for your own records – if you do, ask your coachee's permission first.

Storing your notes

As with any sensitive data, you should always keep your notes securely locked away and ensure you do not allow anyone to view or access them. Not only is this a legal requirement, it will also ensure your coachee continues to trust you.

Mind Mapping

Because of the complex nature of the information coming out of some coaching sessions it can sometimes be difficult to adequately record all of the points. One technique you can use to help create some sense of logic to your notes is called 'mind mapping'.

This is a technique for exploring, brainstorming and representing ideas and, as such, is a particularly useful way of representing all of the main facets of your coaching discussion, especially if you like to see things represented graphically.

Hot tip

Mind mapping is a great way to record all the complex ideas coming from a coaching session.

Drawing a mind map

To draw a mind map, you firstly write or draw a central idea in the middle of a page. Then add linked ideas or topics, drawn radiating from this central idea. You can draw or write these in whatever arrangement or style you think is appropriate. If you want to you can even use pictures.

Each one of these secondary linkages can, again, have further linkages showing the relationship to the last. Here is a simple mind map used to brainstorm possible holiday options:

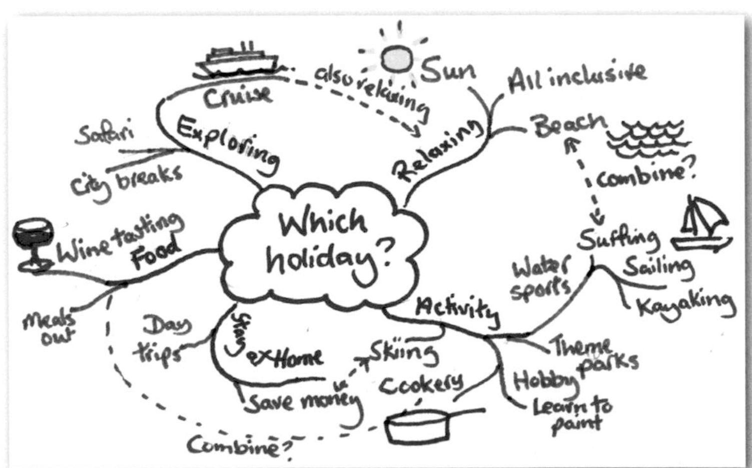

Keep it free flowing

It is best to use blank paper for mind mapping so your maps are kept free flowing and don't turn into linear lists. There is not meant to be any priority assumed by the order and positioning of the ideas. This is useful when you are recording your coachee's ideas because you are not then making any value judgements as you record them.

A coaching example

Applying these principles to coaching, place the ***Aspiration*** as the central idea with each of your coachee's ***Building blocks*** radiating from it. From these will come any sub-divided ***Building blocks***.

We actually showed a simple version of a mind map on page 52 when we were describing ***Building blocks***. Here is a more detailed version as it may appear as part of the coach's notes and based on an aspiration to become a confident presenter. Note that some of the coachee's words have also been recorded in inverted commas and the coachee's chosen ***Building block*** has been asterisked:

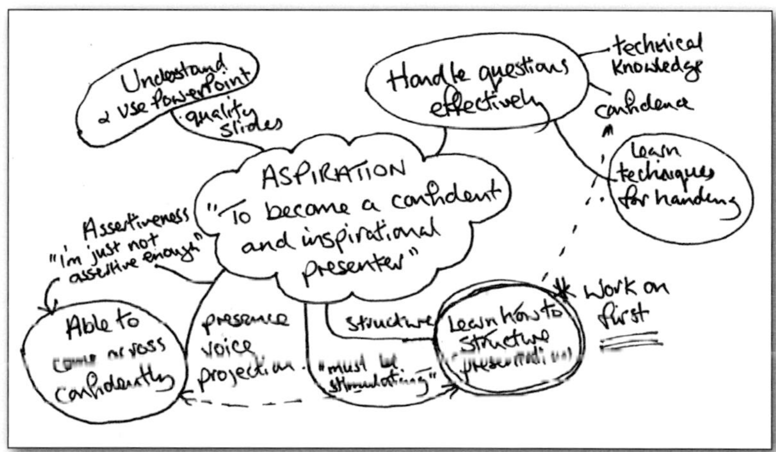

Brainstorming with your coachee

As well as using mind mapping for taking notes, you can also use it as a way of engaging your coachee directly. If you have access to a white board or flip chart, once your coachee has expressed their aspiration, write this in the centre of your space and use it as a focal point for a discussion on all the possible ***Building blocks***.

Seeing this visual representation may help your coachee to see the connections between their ***Aspiration*** and their ***Building blocks*** more clearly and can make the coaching session more dynamic.

Control

Watch, when using this technique, that if you do the writing you do not take over control for the generation of ideas. The normal rule still applies – ask permission before adding your own contributions.

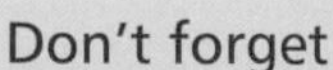

Don't forget

It is your coachee's responsibility to come up with ideas and not the coach's, even when brainstorming.

Summary

- There are two main types of questions – open and closed. Open questions are generally more effective in coaching as they elicit more than just 'yes' or 'no' responses
- High-gain questions are a form of open question. They are particularly useful as they encourage your coachee to give a longer response based on their opinions
- Keeping your questioning conversational will maintain rapport and encourage your coachee to open up more
- Try to avoid using questions starting with 'why' as these force your coachee to have to justify themselves
- Definitely avoid asking leading questions which manipulate your coachee into answering the way you want them to
- Using nods and noises such as 'uh-huh' shows your coachee you are listening and encourages them to continue
- Show your interest by maintaining good eye contact, leaning forward and through your facial expressions
- Active listening involves summarizing and paraphrasing from time to time. It helps you to listen more effectively and also reassures your coachee that you have understood them
- When summarizing, make sure you accurately reflect what your coachee has said and that you don't filter what you hear and so summarize based on your own agenda
- When your coachee uses particularly distinctive words and phrases note them down and, when summarizing, replay them back exactly as they were expressed by your coachee
- You need to keep notes during the meeting but don't stop your coachee's flow to get them down
- Keep your coaching notes securely locked away and never divulge any of the content of your meetings to others
- Mind mapping can be a useful way of recording the meeting but also a way of engaging your coachee when brainstorming their *Building blocks*

6 Setting Goals

Goal-setting plays a crucial role in coaching. There are very few parts of the coaching process that don't in some way utilize goal-setting skills. Apart from the coaching process, goal-setting is also a very important and useful management skill.

92 Goals in Coaching

93 Why Set Goals?

94 Goal-setting Models

95 SMART

96 MARC and Other Derivatives

97 SMART in Coaching

98 Reactions to Goals

99 Personality and Goals

100 SMART in Sport?

102 Visualization

104 Using Visualization

106 Goal-setting Examples

108 Summary

Goals in Coaching

Goals in the coaching process

If you consider each of the stages of our coaching process you will see that goal-setting plays a vital part in almost every stage:

- **Aspirations** – are, of course, your coachee's long-term goals and therefore enhancing your understanding of goal-setting is very relevant for this element
- **Building blocks** – break down the ***Aspiration*** into more achievable sub-goals which, once achieved, will ultimately lead to the accomplishment of your performer's ***Aspiration***
- **Development** – covers a set of actions towards the accomplishment of the chosen ***Building block*** and each can therefore be treated as a mini goal
- **Energize** – the whole essence of ***Energizing*** is to give clarity and motivation to your performer towards completing their actions and therefore this stage is probably the most important part of the goal-setting process
- **Follow up** – the review of your performer's activity and progress to date is part of the measurement of the performer's development plan and therefore, again part of goal-setting

In fact the only stage in our coaching process that doesn't utilise some element of goal-setting is *Current*.

With goal-setting being so integral to the process of coaching it is essential that we consider this important area in more detail.

Hot tip 

Effective goal-setting is an essential process to master, even outside of the coaching process.

Why Set Goals?

Two important elements

There are two main elements to setting effective goals:

1. Ensuring that both you and the performer are clear about what goals have been agreed and what they need to do to achieve them

2. Leaving your performer motivated and confident about the prospect of achieving their goals

Misunderstanding

There is nothing worse than meeting up with someone to review their achievement towards a goal, maybe during a performance review or following a coaching session, only to find that their interpretation of the goal was very different to yours and, as a result, they have worked towards achieving something completely different.

Poorly set goals can result in:

- Wasted effort on the part of the individual who may have devoted considerable time and personal energy towards achieving their interpretation of the goal
- The individual becoming demotivated and cautious about putting effort into any future goals in case the same thing happens again
- Possible duplication of effort if the individual's interpretation has led them to overlap with someone else's responsibilities
- A delay in the completion of the goal which could have a significant impact if some time has elapsed since the goal was originally agreed

Whose goal?

As with all other elements of coaching, when we refer to 'setting' a goal, remember it is the responsibility of your performer to decide on their goals. When *Energizing*, you can help your performer to have clarity over their goal but it is still **their** goal.

We will briefly look into some of the basic psychology behind goal-setting later in this chapter.

In coaching it is the performer who sets their goals and not you.

Goal-setting Models

Why use a model?

Using a standard goal-setting model or process within an organization can help to ensure a consistent approach. It can also act as a memory aid to ensure all the elements of goal-setting have been followed.

All goal-setting models aim to achieve the same outcome – clarity and purpose over the goal being set. They will hopefully avoid any misunderstanding and the resultant impacts we described earlier.

Which model?

Of the various goal-setting models in business, the two most commonly used are based on simple mnemonics or memory aids:

- SMART
- MARC

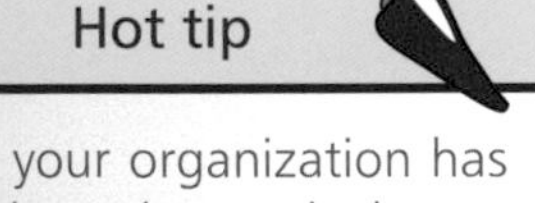

If your organization has adopted a particular goal-setting model, it is probably best to continue to use this one.

Of the two, SMART is probably more commonly adopted but, if your organization has adopted another similar model, then it may be appropriate to continue to use that model within your coaching to maintain consistency.

SMART

For a goal to be clear and well defined it needs to meet each of the following criteria:

SMART

Specific

A goal needs to be specific - that is, it needs to be clearly specified in terms of what is to be accomplished, when and by whom. As a coach you should be listening for vague or general language and then questioning your coachee to establish enough detail for the goal to become clear and understood.

Hot tip 

Listen out for vague language when your performer is defining their goals. Question them where necessary to gain more clarity.

Measurable

A goal must be measurable so that your coachee knows when they have achieved it. Being measurable means being quantifiable – a goal to 'increase sales' is meaningless unless it states by how much. An individual who increases sales by just one item can otherwise say they have accomplished their goal.

Some topics are, by their nature, easier to quantify – sales being a good example. Goals relating to 'softer' topic areas such as leadership behaviors can prove harder to measure but it should still be possible to put measures in place with some careful thought.

Achievable or Attainable

If a goal feels difficult or unattainable, there is a danger that your coachee will feel discouraged and decide, even before starting, not to bother trying. As we shall discuss later, it can be motivating for a goal to be a challenge and can help to stretch the individual but if the goal appears unattainable, it is likely to be demotivating.

Relevant*

If your coachee is to commit to a goal, they need to see the relevance in striving for it and achieving it. Without relevance they will be doing it just for the sake of it and are unlikely, therefore, to fully commit to it.

Timed

Finally, all goals need to be set in the context of a timescale. Over what period of time is the goal to be completed? Without this element the goal may be allowed to drift and, as a result, may not be accomplished.

*You may see some models using 'realistic' in place of 'relevant'. This, for the most part, overlaps with 'achievable' and therefore does not really add anything to the model.

MARC and Other Derivatives

MARC

Another commonly used goal-setting model is MARC which you will note has very similar elements to SMART:

If using this model, you will still need to ensure that the goal is 'specific'; this is not explicitly included as part of this model as is the case with SMART.

Having the term 'controllable' is a useful addition as the performer does need to have control or influence over its completion for it to be a valid goal.

However refined your goal-setting model is you still need to remember to use it!

SMARTER

Beyond the basic SMART mnemonic there have been numerous attempts to enhance or adapt it. One is to add 'ER' to make it SMARTER. This adds the elements 'Excite and Review' but there are also many other derivations. Whatever mnemonic you choose to adopt, the important thing is to use it!

Reviewing goals

However well a goal has been defined, there needs to be a point when it is reviewed to check progress. If you do not review goals, having agreed them, most people will soon start to realize they can get away with not bothering to work at their goals.

Within our coaching process this is picked up as part of the *Follow up* which we shall look at again in Chapter 7.

SMART in Coaching

We stated earlier how important goal-setting was within the coaching process. Now you can use SMART with your coachee to better define the outcomes from each stage.

Aspiration

Within the first stage, *Aspiration,* you can question your coachee about how they can make it more **specific** and more **measurable**. You can test them to establish whether they are being realistic about their ability to **achieve** their aspiration. You can probably assume that their aspiration is **relevant** otherwise they would not have introduced it but you can certainly find out within what **time** period they expect to make their aspiration a reality.

Building blocks

It would be too rigorous and time consuming to apply SMART to each individual *Building block* your coachee lists but, once your coachee has decided which *Building block* they intend to work on first, you can then question them to define it more clearly.

Development and Energize

As with *Building blocks*, you only need to help your coachee to define more clearly their chosen actions. This can be done when *Energizing* your coachee because you will remember that, out of the three elements which make up *Energize*, one is dedicated to firming up on your coachee's chosen actions.

From your coachee

By questioning your coachee, you can encourage them to focus on their goals without imposing your views. If your coachee is also familiar with SMART, you can ask them more explicitly how they can make some of their decisions and actions more SMART.

Hot tip

If your coachee is also familiar with SMART you can both discuss how to best define their goals using the model.

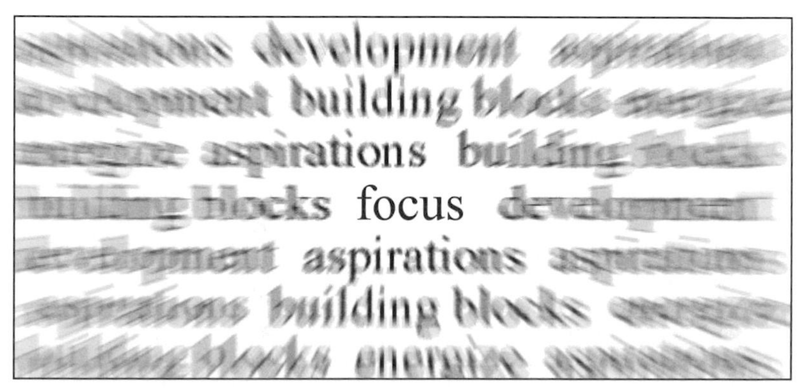

Reactions to Goals

Life would be very straightforward – if a little boring – if everyone reacted in the same way to being set a goal. But of course this isn't the case and therefore, however well-defined and achievable the goals, people will react in many different ways.

Contributing factors

There are many factors which will affect the way your performer is likely to react to a goal, including:

- Their general mindset at the time of setting the goal
- Their previous experience of achieving (or otherwise) the goals they have agreed to
- Other external factors happening around them at the time
- Their underlying personality

Having the right mindset

In Chapter 2 we discussed the importance of ensuring your performer comes to the coaching relationship with a mindset which is positive and 'on receive'.

Providing your performer is taking responsibility for their own goals there should be few issues resulting from the first two of the above factors as they will be in control and setting goals which they feel comfortable with.

Beware 

You may not be aware of external factors which may be affecting how your coachee reacts to their goals.

External factors

However well you think you know your performer, when you sit down with them for a coaching session, you can never know all the things that are happening in their life that could be affecting them at the time.

By highlighting any potential blockages whilst *Energizing*, you can hopefully encourage your performer to, at least, raise some of their main concerns. But be mindful that any number of external factors can get in the way, from their sports team losing last night, the car breaking down, through to a family pet dying!

Personality and Goals

One of the biggest impacts on the reaction of an individual to a goal is their personality. We do not have enough space to delve deeply into this highly complex and fascinating subject but can at least highlight its importance.

Personality and personality types

When we refer to personality, we are describing an individual's enduring characteristics, qualities or behaviors that make them different from someone else.

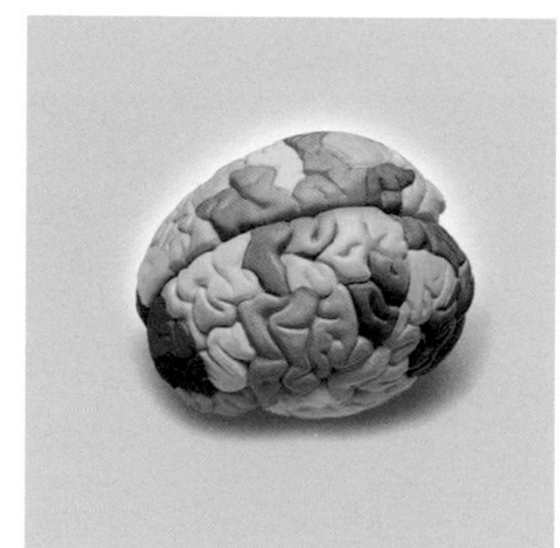

Much work has been done to try to characterize specific personality types – that is, groupings which describe differences in people's psychological makeup.

One example of a personality type instrument is the much-used Myers-Briggs Type Indicator (MBTI). We have provided details on where to find more information on this and other models in Chapter 10.

More recent thinking, however, is moving away from the idea of categorizing people into such simple 'either/or' dimensions as the reality is that people's personalities are far more complex than can be defined by such approaches.

Different reactions

As a result of differences in personality you may find that, whilst some people relish the thought of new challenges and will put a great degree of personal energy into completing a goal, other people will find the same goal either an imposition or possibly even a frightening prospect.

For some, a less challenging goal may encourage them to give it a go whilst others may feel under-challenged and decide to add their own challenges in order to make it more interesting.

The main message is that we are all very different and, as a result, you should be mindful that your performer may react differently to you over the prospect of a particular goal.

Don't forget

Personality can have a big impact on an individual's reaction and willingness to pursue a particular goal.

SMART in Sport?

An unlikely scenario

Imagine you are coaching a top athlete – a pole vaulter – in the final few days before competing at the Olympics. Both of you have been working towards this moment for years and your performer is at the very peak of their fitness and performance levels. All the hours of relentless training mean they have every chance of winning a medal if not a gold.

So, with just days to go, you decide to focus your performer by setting a goal for this ultimate event. Being a strong proponent of SMART, here's what you decide to say to your performer:

"As you know, on Tuesday 27 July you will be competing in the pole vault finals and you can certainly expect to achieve a medal position. Given your current performance levels I think you should aim to achieve a height of 6.04 metres which is just two centimeters more than your current personal best."

It meets all of the SMART criteria. It's specific and is definitely measurable. You know the height is within their grasp. Clearly it is relevant and you even have the date when you expect it to be achieved. In fact, it couldn't be more SMART!

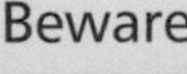

Beware

Just because a goal meets all the SMART criteria won't necessarily make it inspiring.

Inspiring your performer

There is no way, however, that this goal would inspire your performer towards achieving their gold medal. What is missing is any form of motivation or excitement about what needs to be achieved.

Yet, in business, we somehow expect that by relying on a model such as SMART, this level of goal-setting is going to work.

Of course, sports coaches will ensure any goal that is agreed meets a set of criteria such as SMART but they will want to be far more engaging than this to truly motivate their performer.

An alternative scenario

Let's re-run the scenario again, but this time you will motivate your performer by describing the event in far more detail:

"As you know, on Tuesday you are going to be competing in the pole vault finals and we both know you have every chance of achieving a gold medal this time.

Put yourself in the stadium on that afternoon – there is a roar from the crowd after the end of the 400 meter final. You can sense all eyes are now on you as you make your final jump of 6.04 meters.

You are completely focussed and, as the crowd quietens, all you can hear and feel is your heart beating. You blank your mind to the crowd and as you set off on your run you are working every fiber of every muscle to its full capacity.

You engage your pole in the pit and already know your timing and take-off are perfect. You put every last drop of energy into this jump because you know this is the one that counts. As you see your legs swing up and you arch your body over the bar you already know you are well clear and the gold medal is yours."

Visualization

The above version still contains all the elements of the SMART goal-setting model but is likely to have far more impact and leave your performer with a more positive attitude towards achieving their goal.

It describes the goal using 'visualization techniques'. We will now describe how you can also use these in your coaching sessions and in other management situations to enhance the way you set goals.

Visualization

Hot tip

Athletes and coaches use visualization techniques – using strong and positive images to bring to life their goals.

Many top athletes use visualization or visioning techniques in preparation for important competitions. By enacting a future performance in their mind using strong and positive images to make it as real as possible, a performer can experience far more vividly how they are going to achieve their goal.

All the senses

When we talk about visualization we are actually referring to the enactment or re-enactment in our minds based on:

- What we will see (visual)
- What we will hear (auditory)
- What we will feel (kinesthetic)
- And sometimes even based on what we will smell or taste

These are obviously our five main senses and by using these senses within our visualization we are able to recreate the situation in our mind as if we are actually experiencing it.

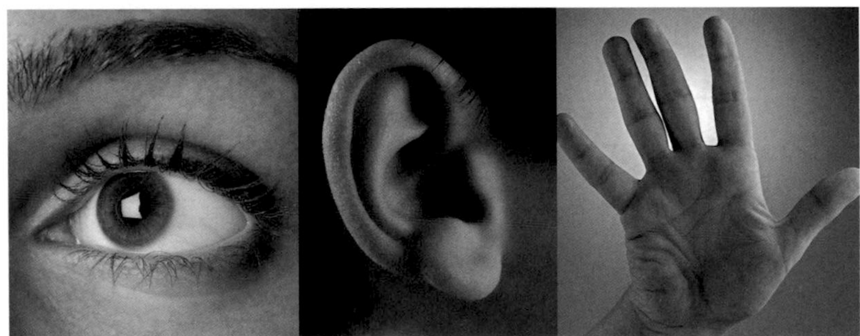

Trigger words and phrases

Referring back to our second scenario where you were preparing your pole vaulter for the Olympics, you will see words and phrases within the description which were designed to trigger all three of the main senses:

"There is a roar from the crowd..." (Auditory)

"...all you can hear and feel is your heart beating" (Auditory and Kinesthetic)

"As you see your legs swing up..." (Visual)

Thinking styles

When you think about a situation, whether in the past or in the future, you use a combination of visual, auditory or kinesthetic 'images', known as thinking styles. We should point out that the term 'kinesthetic' is used to mean feeling and refers to both our emotional feeling as well as our sense of feeling or touch.

Images in your mind

So, if you are now asked to think about going out to a restaurant for a meal with friends, you will probably be able to conjure up pictures or even a moving image of this scenario in your mind – hence the expression 'mind's eye'. You are thinking **visually**.

You should also be able to imagine the sounds of your friends talking and the clattering of plates and glasses clinking. These are based on **auditory** thinking.

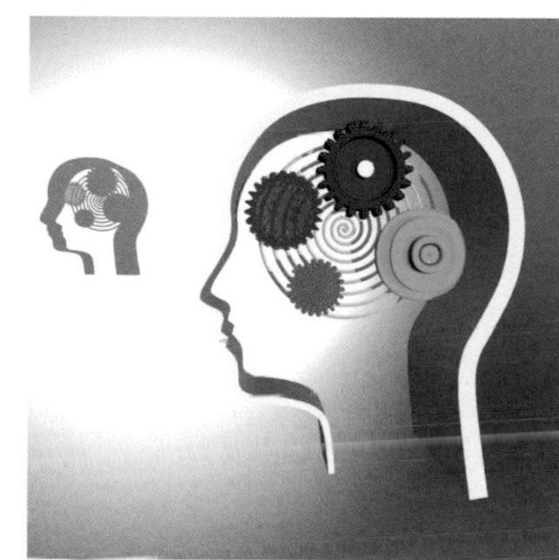

If you can bring to mind how you are feeling emotionally, as well as textures such as the feel of food in your mouth or, say, the texture of the table cloth you are using a **kinesthetic** thinking style.

Given the scenario, you may also be able to bring into your mind the smells and tastes of your food and drink.

Dominant style

Even though you may be able to bring all of these senses into your mind you will most likely have one sense that is more dominant than the others.

Given this, when using visioning, you always need to be aware that your performer's dominant thinking style may not necessarily be the same as yours.

As we shall see, it is important to either adapt your visioning to tap into your performer's dominant thinking style or try to use all of the senses in your visioning.

Don't forget

Be mindful when visualizing that your coachee may have a different dominant thinking style to you.

Using Visualization

The words we use

When we talk, we tend to naturally use words which we associate with our more dominant sensory styles. Here are some examples:

- **Visual** – I *see* what you mean – Let's *focus* on that
- **Auditory** – That *sounds* like a good idea – That *rings a bell*
- **Kinesthetic** – It *feels* like the right thing to do

By listening to the language your performer is using you may be able to determine which is their dominant style.

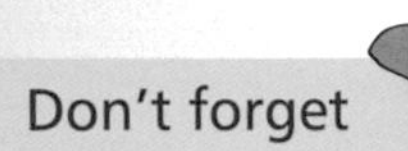

Don't forget

Your coachee may have a different dominant thinking style to yours so try to use a range of visioning styles.

Visualization in goal-setting

When you visualize within goal-setting you should remember the other person may have a different dominant thinking style to yours. Unless you know their dominant style you should use a range of descriptors that pick up on all the senses, as we did in our pole vaulting example.

A business example

Let us now take a business goal example and see how it can be enhanced by visualizing. Firstly, here is the standard SMART goal:

"So we are agreed that by next Friday you will have completed your analysis and have prepared your draft project plan for me to look over – the first time you will have done this on your own."

Now let's take the same goal and make it more motivating by adding some visualization:

"So this is your chance to really shine. Next Friday I hope to see a pleased look on your face when you hand me your first draft project plan. We both know you are excellent at analysis and so I can imagine you'll eat up the data analysis with no problem. Just take your time when preparing the plan itself – crystallize your thoughts first so it's clear in your mind. I'm already looking forward to hearing how you got on."

Visualization within our coaching process

In one sense, adding visualization into our coaching is easier. Instead of you having to create a vision, you can question your coachee to encourage them to come up with their own images. To encourage your coachee to visualize their aspiration you can ask questions such as:

- Put yourself at the point of having reached your aspiration. Describe what it feels like – what do you see?
- Just stop for a minute and tell me more about what that aspiration will be like when you finally achieve it

Of course, if your coachee already knows about visualizing, you can ask them directly:

- Let's stop and think about your aspiration. Visualize yourself achieving it and then tell me what you see, hear or feel.

Accentuating the positive

One point we have not discussed relates to negative thoughts. So far we have concentrated on the positive benefits of visualization but negative thoughts and visualizing can be a big problem, particularly for sports people.

Your coachee can just as easily visualize themselves failing to achieve their goal, putting themselves in a negative mindset. As a result, they are more likely to fail.

Thoughts such as "I can't do that" or "I knew I would fail" can be very destructive and it is therefore important that you encourage your coachee to concentrate only on positive images.

Hot tip

Encourage your coachee to visualize their aspirations by asking them questions.

Beware

Watch that your coachee doesn't start to visualize negative thoughts and images of failing.

Goal-setting Examples

On the following two pages are examples showing how goal-setting and visualization can be used to good effect within your coaching meetings. In real situations you would have time to explore each one with your performer in much more detail:

If your meeting is relaxed and conversational you will get an open response by starting with "Tell me...".

Example 1 – Aspirations

Performer: I've always wanted to start my own business.

Coach: Put yourself in the position where that's become reality – what's that like?

Performer: Well, ideally, it would be my own accountancy firm. I wouldn't want to be just on my own so I would need to find someone to come in with me as a partner.

Coach: So put yourself in your new office – tell me about the things you're doing, the people around you and how you're feeling.

Performer: I would have a small office with two or three people... maybe a reception for clients. It won't be for another five years or so because I need to finish my qualifications first. It won't be anything too fancy but I think I will concentrate on small traders in the area. It would be really busy with people coming in and out all the time - a real buzz about it! I could imagine being really proud of that.

Example 2 – Building blocks

Performer: The building block I want to work on first is to become more organized.

Coach: How would you like things to be ideally? – describe 'more organized' when it's all working as you would like it to be.

Performer: Ideally I want to get to a point where I don't have all these huge piles of work on my desk and I'd know exactly where everything is. Someone could come up to my desk and I will be able to reach across and find the file straight away. Most importantly, I won't need to get so flustered and tense.

Coach: By when would you like it to be like that?

Performer: Well, not more than a month from now.

(The measure in this last example is that the individual will be sufficiently organized to be able to find a file straight away.)

Example 3 – Development and Energize

Performer: One action I'm going to work on is practicing asking open questions.

Coach: So talk me through you actually doing that.

Performer: I will have to ask a colleague to help and find some time when we are both free. Maybe I could book a room for half an hour next week. I will ask her to think of a coaching topic in advance and then I can ask her questions and focus on making sure they are all open questions.

Coach: Be more precise in your description, describe the detail of you actually doing it – for example, who with? And how will you know if you are asking good questions?

Performer: I'll ask Chris if she will help because she is pretty good at questioning. I know Chris will be able to tell me if I'm asking good questions. I'll book a room for next week for an hour. I want to make it as real as possible so I'll introduce it as if it were a real coaching session and build rapport just as I would for real.

Coach: That sounds great. We want to make sure that nothing gets in the way of this happening so walk yourself through you actually doing this in your mind and, as you do so, tell me of anything which could stop it from happening.

Performer: The only thing I can think of which could stop it is if Chris is not free next week.

Coach: So how will you deal with that?

Performer: I would be prepared to wait a few more days if next week turns out to be a problem. But I do want to get this done so if not, I will ask Jim instead.

Don't forget

Using visualization is a great way to get your coachee to imagine what blockages might stop them completing their actions.

Summary

- Goal-setting appears in all stages of the coaching process with the exception of ***Current***
- Without a well-defined goal your performer will not know when they have achieved the desired level or may spend energy on the wrong activity
- It is useful to use a goal-setting model such as SMART or MARC. This will ensure their goal is clear and understood
- When focusing on goals within coaching you can encourage your performer to describe and set their own goals by asking open questions
- People react differently to goals so don't assume your performer will react to a goal the same way as you would
- A number of factors can affect your performer's reaction to a goal including how well they have accomplished previous goals as well as external influences in their home life
- Our personalities also play an important part in how we react to goals
- Using a goal-setting model such as SMART is important but goals can be made more motivational through the use of visualization techniques
- Visioning or visualization involves the vivid enactment of a scenario in our minds based on our senses – especially what we see, hear and feel
- Introducing visioning into the coaching process involves asking your performer questions to encourage them to describe their goal
- We each have a dominant thinking style and, as a result, our performer may not share your same thinking style. As a coach you will need to ask questions triggering all of the senses
- It is important to keep your performer's mindset positive because negative visioning can result in them focusing on failing

7 Ongoing Coaching

Coaching is based on a long-term relationship. Knowing how to progress the relationship and understanding the various options available to you at different stages in that relationship will ensure you and your coachee keep on track and they ultimately achieve their aspiration.

110 Reviewing Progress
111 Transfer to the Real World
112 Reviewing Current
113 Dealing with Slow Progress
114 Changing Plans
115 The Next Building Block
116 Starting the Process Again
118 Follow-up Meeting Format
120 The Ongoing Relationship
122 Evaluating Progress
124 Evaluation in Practice
125 Observing Your Coachee
126 Summary

Reviewing Progress

In Chapter 4 we explored the basic outline of what needs to be discussed during a follow-up meeting. We will now explore follow-up meetings in more detail and, in particular, the various options open to you and your performer depending on their progress.

What to discuss

At the end of your last meeting you will have decided a date for the next follow-up meeting, probably based on your performer having completed their chosen set of actions or at least having reached a significant point. Your focus, for the first part of the meeting, will therefore be on what they have done and what they have learned from their activity.

Your performer's review

As we have previously described, on the basis your performer has taken responsibility for their development they should be keen to tell you how they have progressed since the last meeting. Encourage them to provide a balanced view of both the positive and any negative outcomes.

Good questions to ask

Having heard your performer's review, there is probably still merit in questioning your performer to help them focus on the key learning points and so gain the most from the experience. Here are some questions to ask. The first is a closed question, the second an open and the third a high-gain question:

- Did the exercise do what you wanted it to do?
- When you say the book/exercise/role play was useful, what were the main learning points for you?
- How has this progressed your understanding?

Learning from things that go wrong

It is possible that not everything your performer attempts will work. Even seemingly negative experiences can be turned into useful learning opportunities by asking your performer questions such as:

- Even though you didn't feel it worked, what did you still learn from at least giving it a try?
- What will you do differently next time?

Even an unsuccessful action can have positive outcomes by exploring what your coachee has learned.

Transfer to the Real World

It is important when your performer carries out development away from the job that they can see how what they have learned applies to their role or the achievement of their ***Building block***.

Hot tip

It is important to make sure your coachee sees the link between the learning experience and their role.

Direct application

Some of your performer's development actions will have a direct application within a work context. For instance, practicing new questioning skills or trying out new delegation techniques. For these the link is probably self-evident.

Indirect application

Other development actions may be only small pieces of a much larger jigsaw and therefore the link between the activities and how they are used in the context of your performer's ***Building block*** may need to be made. For instance:

- Reading a book or article covering the underpinning knowledge to a given skill or behavior
- Observing someone seen as an expert in a given activity
- Training someone else on a topic to consolidate your performer's own learning

It is important your questioning helps your performer understand these links between their development activity and their role. Here are a couple of examples of questions you can use – the first is a good high-gain question:

- How will what you have read so far benefit you in your role?
- From what you have learned, what have you already applied into your day-to-day work? How did this go?

Reviewing Current

Since the last meeting, your coachee will have been working on development actions, which they chose, to hopefully close the development gap between where they believed they were – ***Current***, in our model – and where they need to be to achieve their chosen ***Building block***.

In reviewing progress we are, effectively, returning to our coaching model to reassess your coachee's current state.

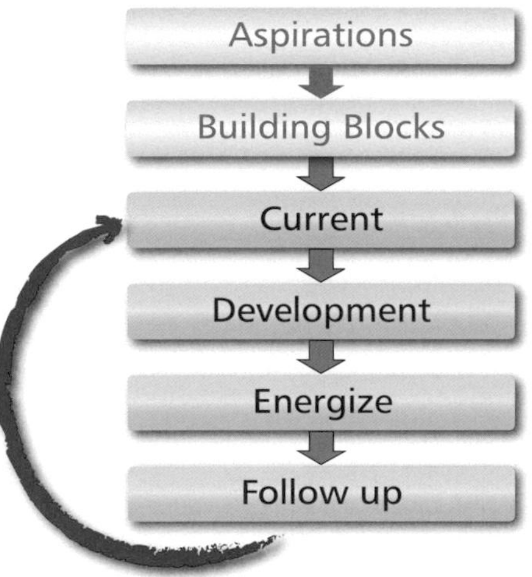

Little by little

Having worked on these actions, your coachee's ***Current*** position should have now changed. Hopefully this will be in a positive direction but it may only be a slight change or improvement. Your role as coach is to notice these small changes and bring them to the attention of your coachee.

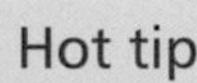

Hot tip

Don't worry if at first your coachee's skill level drops. It shows they have been trying something new.

Going backwards

Sometimes trying out new skills and behaviors can initially result in an individual going backwards in skill level. This is nothing to worry about.

From the skill development model we outlined in Chapter 1 you should recall that your coachee may at first need to go through the discomfort of realizing their lack of competence before then developing their competence level. Reassure your coachee that many new skills only become second nature after a great degree of practice and regular usage.

Dealing with Slow Progress

Your coachee may report they have not progressed as quickly as they had expected or they may have not completed their development actions at all. If this is the case, but they are still generally happy to continue with their current actions, you may just need to set a new date to meet again to review progress once they have completed their actions.

Of course, if your coachee has made some progress it may still be worth discussing with them how they have progressed so far. There may be some learning as a result of even this small amount of progress.

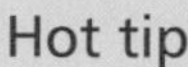

Hot tip

If your coachee has not completed their actions you may just need to re-diarize to meet again.

Re-energize

If your coachee's slow progress is as a result of an unforeseen blockage or, perhaps, a lack of motivation towards their chosen actions, it is worth exploring why this is.

Remember not to put your coachee on the defensive by asking lots of 'why' questions. You may just need to re-energize your coachee or you could consider adapting their actions to make them more motivating and interesting.

Still no progress

If after a couple of follow-up meetings your coachee still hasn't completed any of their development actions you may need to probe further to find out the causes. Their reasons may be genuine but it could be something more fundamental regarding their attitude towards being coached

Changing Plans

Your performer may have attempted their development actions as planned but found that they did not have the desired outcome. This could be as a result of any of the following:

- The development actions were not aligned closely enough to the desired skills to deliver the anticipated outcome. If this is the case you may just need to brainstorm again some alternative development actions, learning from the last attempt
- Your performer is having difficulty learning the desired skills or behaviors and needs more opportunity to practice. It may be a matter of giving your performer more time for the learning to work
- Your performer has a 'mental block' and doesn't believe they can do it. This needs more investigation to help your performer understand what is holding them back before determining the best way forward

Whatever the reason, once you have decided on the best way forward, you will need to ***Energize*** again, as you would have done with their original set of development actions, before agreeing a date and time to meet up again.

If your coachee has made progress, use the opportunity to note their progress and congratulate them.

Success

Of course, the ideal outcome is that your performer has successfully completed their development actions and, as a result, has partly or completely achieved their chosen ***Building block***.

Where this is the case remember to praise your performer's success which will help maintain their motivation towards achieving their ultimate ***Aspiration***.

We will now look at what happens when your performer has completed their ***Building block*** and their options at this point.

The Next Building Block

Provided your performer is committed to their development actions they will eventually start making progress towards the achievement of their chosen *Building block*.

If the *Building block* is relatively straightforward, this may be possible after completing just one set of development actions. For more complex or larger *Building blocks* your performer may need to set and complete a number of development actions over several coaching sessions before they achieve their desired level.

Eventually your performer will know, from the measures they determined initially, that they have completed their *Building block* – an important milestone to celebrate!

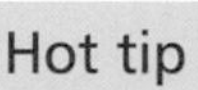

Hot tip

If your coachee has put in place clear measures, they will know when they have achieved their *Building block*.

What next?

So, having completed this *Building block,* it is now time to move on to the next and so move one important step closer towards your performer achieving their aspiration.

At this point, it is time to refer back to your notes and the original conversation regarding *Building blocks* to decide which one to tackle next. In effect, in our coaching process, we are now looping back up to *Building blocks*:

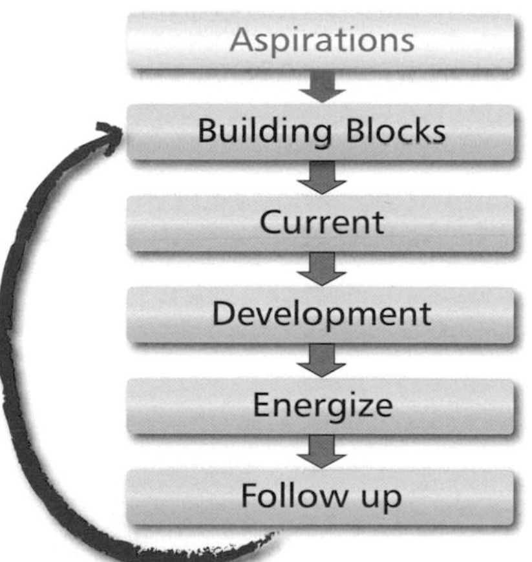

List of Building blocks

If necessary, remind your performer of their list of *Building blocks* created in the first meeting. It is worth checking that they still feel this list is accurate in case they have now thought of others.

Starting the Process Again

Just as you did in the first meeting, you need to discuss with your performer which *Building block* is the most appropriate to work on next. You may need to remind them of the various factors that will determine the best *Building block* to choose next.

Following the model

From this point on, your follow up session should mirror a full coaching meeting:

- **Current** – Establish through questioning, your performer's current level of capability relating to the newly chosen *Building block*
- **Development** – Brainstorm all the possible development actions which will help close the development gap
- **Energize** – *Energize* your performer ensuring you leave them with a clear plan, motivated and knowing how they will deal with any potential blockages

Once your performer has a new development plan based on their next *Building block* you can agree a date for a follow-up meeting and so the process starts all over again.

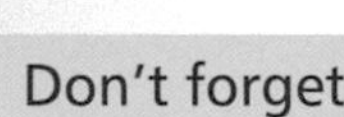
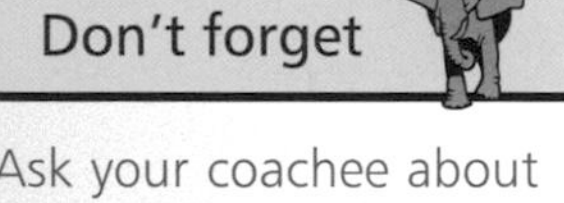

Don't forget

Ask your coachee about their aspiration from time to time so they are reminded of the WIIFM –what's in it for me.

Aspiration reminder

With all this activity around *Building blocks* it is easy to lose sight of the ultimate goal – achievement of your performer's aspiration.

It is worth reminding your performer of their aspiration from time to time, particularly at the point of starting a new *Building block*. Question your performer to check whether it is still relevant or whether they have adapted their views given the experiences they have gained so far.

Change in Aspiration

When your performer describes and visualizes their long-term goal during the first meeting they will have based this on their best understanding of its realism and viability at the time.

By exploring all the necessary ***Building blocks*** needed to reach this aspiration your performer will already have a sense-check over how difficult or easy this will be to reach.

But as the coaching progresses, you may find your performer chooses to re-evaluate their aspiration, either to raise the bar further or to lower their sights.

Lowering their sights

Your performer may decide their aspiration was unrealistic and is no longer something they want to aim for. Before just agreeing with them, question your performer to establish whether this is just as a result of a temporary loss of confidence or self-belief because they have hit a difficult patch.

It is good to question your performer over this but it is not your role to tell them they must or should continue with this aspiration.

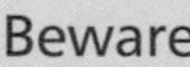
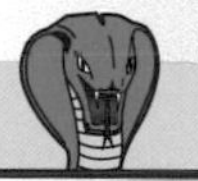

Beware

If your coachee decides their aspiration is too high, question them to find out if this is because of a loss of confidence.

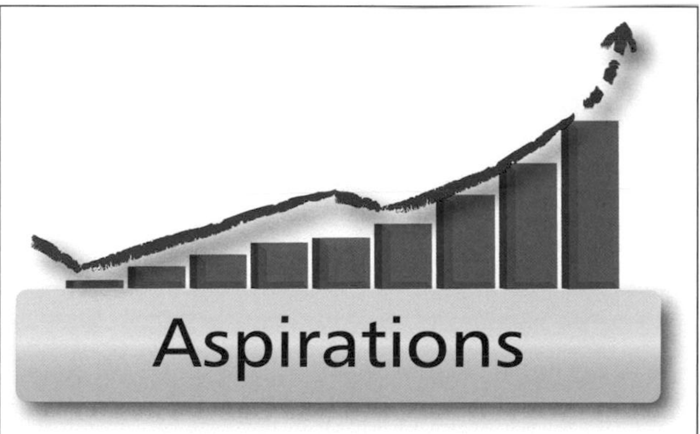

Raising the bar

More likely your performer will start to get some successes under their belt and will start progressing as a result. As your performer builds in confidence you could find they want to aim higher than they originally targeted themselves. This is clearly great news and a sign that the coaching is having a positive effect.

Follow-up Meeting Format

As we described in Chapter 3, a first coaching meeting can last anywhere between one and two hours... perhaps even longer if the issues discussed are complex.

Follow-up meetings can vary considerably in time scale. A short follow-up meeting to discuss progress and reset development actions may only need half an hour.

As we have described, a follow-up meeting may result in your coachee concluding their current *Building block*. This will mean going back into the coaching process to determine the next *Building block* to work on, putting in place a new development plan and then energizing your coachee. This may obviously take more time.

Hot tip 

If you weren't anticipating having to start work on a new building block it may be better to reconvene rather than rush it.

Book a new meeting

If you had not anticipated that this was going to be the case, you may decide, having reviewed your coachee's progress and finished with the old *Building block*, to agree a date to reconvene. This way you can ensure you dedicate sufficient time to work on the next *Building block*.

Non judging

As with all your coaching meetings, keep the follow-up meeting relaxed. Whether your coachee has made great progress or not, avoid becoming judgmental. Your role is to focus their thinking so that they can effectively analyze their own experiences and therefore decide their next steps.

If your coachee has clearly made no attempt towards their development actions there may be perfectly justifiable reasons. You can easily discover this through careful questioning.

Corridor coaching

Sometimes you can conduct a 'mini' follow-up meeting while passing in the corridor just to check out how things are going. It may go something like this:

Coach: Hi Chris, I'm glad I bumped into you. How's your development plan going?

Performer: Not bad. I managed to get a copy of that book on delegation from the local book shop and I'm about half-way through reading it already.

Coach: What do you think, from what you have read so far?

Performer: I've found it really useful and I've even tried putting some of the ideas into practice with my team.

Coach: That's good to hear. So what ideas in particular have you tried so far?

Performer: Well you may remember that one thing I struggled with was who best to give specific responsibilities to. This book has given me some useful guidance on how to do this and I've already used these ideas three or four times.

Coach: Excellent! What about your other action to shadow Jim?

Performer: To be honest, I've not looked at that because I've found more use from the ideas in the book.

Coach: That's fine – so shall we still leave our next follow-up meeting in the diary as planned?

Confidentiality

Of course, this sort of conversation is only possible if you cannot be overheard and the subject is not sensitive but it can be a quick and simple way of catching up on progress.

Hot tip 

An informal update when passing can be a great way to get a quick update on your coachee's progress.

The Ongoing Relationship

If, in your first meeting, your coachee identifies a truly long-term aspiration, you can expect it to take them considerable time to achieve it. After completion of each ***Building block*** your coachee will start another and so on until, hopefully, they finally achieve their aspiration.

Your relationship with your coachee based on one aspiration could last for many months if not years. This assumes, of course, your coachee doesn't decide to amend their aspiration and aim for a higher goal. Even a more focused aspiration such as wanting to become better organized could take several weeks to achieve.

If you are the coachee's manager you can use coaching as part of an ongoing coaching relationship.

Manager relationship

If you are the performer's manager you will most likely want to coach an individual as part of your ongoing management relationship. In this situation, even if your coachee completes a more focused aspiration, there is nothing to stop you then determining a further aspiration and continuing the relationship.

Passing on to another manager

Of course your coachee may get promoted or moved from your team – hopefully as a result of successful coaching! In this situation you need to determine how best to support your coachee following the move.

It may be expected that your coachee's new manager will continue coaching them where you left off. If this is the case, you will need to gain your coachee's permission before handing over any notes. A good way to deal with this is to arrange a hand-over meeting between you, your coachee and their new manager.

Uniformity of approach

Ideally, when a coachee changes coach, they should feel they can continue their development with their new coach as they had done with you. It is clearly best, therefore, if the coachee's new manager also follows the same process as you so that they are in a position to pick up where you left off with the minimum of disruption to the coaching process.

Continuing as their coach

If your relationship with your coachee is a strong and positive one you may agree to continue coaching them even after they moved to work for a different manager. The advantage of this is that, at least in the short term, there will be continuity in the coaching process for your coachee.

There is, however, a significant disadvantage in this arrangement in that the coachee's new manager will not have the opportunity to develop a close relationship and gain a better understanding of their new team member through coaching them.

Beware 

If you continue to coach someone who is now working for another manager, the new manager does not get the opportunity to build a close relationship.

Beyond coaching

Having reached a particular point in the coaching process, you may need to end a coaching relationship - maybe you have been acting as an external coach and agreed to provide a specified number of sessions or perhaps you only agreed to coach an individual until they had achieved a specific aspiration.

In this situation you need to complete the coaching relationship positively leaving your coachee feeling empowered to continue with their own development.

During your final meeting it is worth spending time discussing with your coachee how they will manage their own development. If possible, stress that you are still available to act as a sounding board if they need it.

Evaluating Progress

At the end, and possibly at intervals during the coaching process, you will want to evaluate whether the coaching is having the desired outcome.

At the end of Chapter 2 we discussed the need to consider evaluation right at the beginning of the process. With all the attention around the coaching itself it is all too easy to forget to actually measure how things are going.

For any development activity there are four levels of evaluation you can consider:

- **Level 1 – Was the learning activity interesting and enjoyable for the learner?**

When attending a training course this is usually measured by asking learners to complete 'end of course' evaluation forms. In coaching you can check whether your coachee found their development actions interesting and enjoyable. Whilst this is useful to know, this level of evaluation is probably the least useful for the purposes of coaching.

Beware 

Don't place too much importance on level 1 measures. They only show whether the coachee found it a good experience.

- **Level 2 – Did the individual actually learn anything through completing the development activity?**

This is a more useful measure than level one and, at least, shows that the actions your coachee embarked upon had some benefit. The easiest way to establish this is to question your coachee about what they learned using some of the questions we described earlier in this chapter.

- **Level 3 – What skills or behaviors has the learner started using in their work as a result of their development?**

In terms of coaching, this level of evaluation is an important one. It will indicate whether your coachee's development actions are starting to make a difference in their day-to-day work.

You can evaluate this anecdotally by asking your coachee what changes they have made in the way they do things. To measure this more robustly you could get your coachee to collect evidence of their changed behaviors or gain their permission for you or someone else to observe them using their new skills or behaviors.

- **Level 4 – What bottom-line business improvements have resulted from the learner's changed behaviors?**

This brings us right back to the original business benefit coaching can bring. It can sometimes be difficult to say with certainty that business gains are directly as a result of coaching activity but, ultimately, if the area of coaching directly relates to the business you should be able to monitor the resultant business improvement.

Time delay

When setting in place any form of evaluation you need to be mindful of the time delay between the activity happening and it showing as any tangible change. Clearly, evaluation of both levels 1 and 2 can occur immediately after the activity – your coachee should be able to tell you whether they enjoyed the experience and whether they learned anything straight away.

It may take a little longer to make any meaningful sense at level 3, especially as there may initially be a drop-off in skill level before they improve.

Seeing any tangible changes at level 4 may take several months before behavioral changes make a difference at a business level.

Diarize the evaluation

Given this time delay, if you are planning on evaluating at either level 3 or 4, it is best to diarize when you need to measure the expected changes. This way you will remember to evaluate at the right time. You just need to estimate how long you believe it will take for any changes to filter through to tangible outputs.

Hot tip

Level 3 evaluation of changes your coachee has applied in the work environment are useful indicators.

Beware

Diarize when you need to evaluate any changes otherwise there is a chance both of you will forget.

Evaluation in Practice

The Hawthorne effect

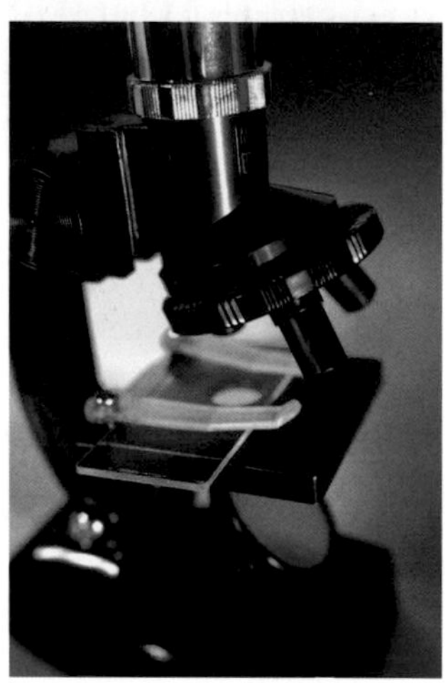

You should be aware that sometimes just the mere fact that you are measuring someone's performance can result in them improving. Their improvement may be more a response to you focusing on their performance rather than the impact of any developmental activity and is known as the 'Hawthorne effect'.

Of course, any improvement is not a bad thing but you should factor this into your evaluation before claiming it is all the result of coaching.

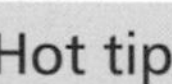

Hot tip 

Keep any evaluation simple and preferably based on existing systems and measures.

Keep it simple

Evaluation is important to ensure the time, effort and money invested in coaching is worthwhile. However, when evaluation becomes too complex, it can actually cost more to administer than the benefits being measured. It can also be demotivating for your coachee if they feel they are being continuously monitored.

Try to keep any evaluation simple and preferably based on existing measures and indicators rather than having to create new systems.

Examples

Here are some example measures for evaluating levels 3 and 4:

- Observing your coachee managing meetings, making presentations, conducting sales or negotiations
- Physically measuring the height of piles of work or the number of emails still unopened in your coachee's inbox
- Asking those who report directly to your coachee to complete questionnaires before and after coaching (with your coachee's permission)
- Monitoring the number of customer complaints or compliments received relating to the activity
- Measuring the increase in sales revenues or a decrease in relevant budgetary expenditure

Observing Your Coachee

A good way to measure level 3, behavioral changes, is for you or a colleague to observe your coachee both to evaluate their behavioral changes and also to feed back to them your observations.

Observing your coachee needs to be done with sensitivity and with their full agreement. Simply ask your coachee how they believe you can jointly evaluate the impact of the coaching. You will then need to also agree with your coachee exactly what they want you to observe.

Keeping inconspicuous

If you have agreed to observe your coachee during a meeting or presentation, preferably choose one you were due to attend anyway. Don't make it obvious to others what you are doing and try to interact as you would normally during the meeting.

Beware 

Don't make it obvious to others in a meeting that you are observing your coachee.

Keeping observation notes

If possible, make notes which record specific instances and best illustrate your observations. Try to capture words and phrases your coachee uses, as well as notes of mannerisms or body language if applicable. This will help when you feed back.

Feeding back

As usual, after the event ask your coachee's permission to feed back your observations. Keep your feedback balanced and always back up your observations with evidence you have collected.

Using another observer

Your coachee may prefer to choose someone else to observe them. This may be someone they regard as an expert or who will provide an alternative viewpoint. You or your coachee will need to brief them on what they are to observe.

Summary

- Question your coachee about their development actions to find out how they have managed and how what they have learned will help them towards achieving their building block
- Don't expect big changes every time. Look out for the small steps forward and bring them to your coachee's attention
- Sometimes your coachee may go backwards in terms of their ability or confidence levels. This may be a good sign and indicates that they are at least trying something different
- If your coachee has not completed their actions you may just need to agree to give them more time and decide another time to meet
- When your coachee believes they have achieved a ***Building block*** they will need to decide which one to work on next and so you return to the coaching process
- It is worth checking, from time to time, that your coachee's aspiration still remains the same
- Corridor coaching can be a good way to quickly catch up on your coachee's progress provided you cannot be overheard
- When handing over coaching to a new manager try to ensure there is minimal disruption for your coachee
- If finishing a coaching relationship, make sure you leave your coachee empowered to continue with their own personal development
- Evaluation can occur at a number of levels but those relating to behavioral change are probably the most useful
- Remember to diarize when you plan to evaluate progress as this may need to be some time after the coaching activity has taken place
- Keep evaluation simple. Try to base it on existing systems and measurements
- When observing your coachee, it needs to be with their consent. Do it inconspicuously and, if possible, in a meeting you are attending anyway

8 The Second Dimensions

The second dimensions bring an added refinement and flexibility to the coaching process and make it possible for you to bring in some of the organization's perspective if needed. Most importantly, it does so without taking the responsibility away from your coachee.

128 About the 2nd Dimensions

130 The Coaching Environment

132 Using the 2nd Dimensions

134 Aspirations

136 Dealing with Differences

138 Building Blocks

140 Current

142 Development

144 Energize

146 Follow up

148 Putting it All Together

150 Summary

About the 2nd Dimensions

Adding to the coaching process

What we have so far described in terms of our coaching process works... exactly as it has been described. It is a very well tried and tested method used for coaching individuals, at all levels, across a wide range of roles and business sectors.

Having said that, there may be times when you may need more flexibility to adapt your coaching style to suit particular situations.

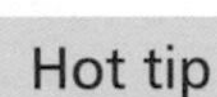

Hot tip

Before trying out the 2nd dimensions, make sure you are comfortable using the core coaching process.

Consolidate first

Before moving on to practice any of the ideas we are about to describe in this chapter, we recommend that you become familiar with and have tried coaching based on the core coaching process as we described in Chapter 4.

What we are about to describe is merely adding refinement and flexibility to the coaching process and, as it may take a while before you feel comfortable adding the second dimensions to your coaching, the core model will work very well as it stands.

Leadership and coaching styles

In Chapter 1 we described the concept of using different leadership and coaching styles and, in particular, that your coaching style needs to be flexible to suit the situation and the individual. The style of coaching we have been recommending falls to the left hand end of our style spectrum, and we described this as hands-off and empowering.

Throughout the book so far, we have stressed the importance of empowering your coachee – asking them questions to encourage them to take responsibility for their own development. For each step of the coaching process, from A through to F, we have suggested questions you could ask to generate responsibility from within your coachee.

Hands-off style best

Remember that a hands-off style is particularly appropriate for individuals who you can trust to take responsibility, for those who have some level of experience and for situations which require creativity or flexibility rather than a prescribed approach.

Given the nature of your coaching sessions, a hands-off style is therefore likely to be by far the most appropriate for you to adopt for most situations. But if the model holds true, there may also be a few occasions where you need to adapt your coaching to a different style.

Bringing in other styles

Our addition of the second dimensions provides a structured way to bring other leadership or coaching styles into our coaching process to match the situation and the individual.

This is not just a matter of letting the coaching session become a training session or an opportunity for you to start giving advice and guidance. To do this would very likely result in your coachee handing back responsibility and becoming a passive recipient rather than a willing participant.

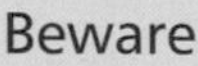
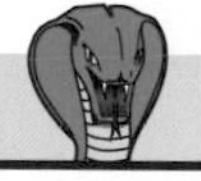

Beware

Don't use the second dimensions as an excuse to use a directive or instructive style.

Not just extremes

Remember the coaching and leadership styles model represents a spectrum of styles moving from hands-off at one extreme to directive at the other. Just because you find yourself in a situation where you need to move away from a hands-off style does not necessarily mean moving to the other extreme. You may only need to adapt your style very slightly to get the desired outcome.

The Coaching Environment

The introduction of coaching

The introduction of sports coaching into the business environment probably began in the mid 1970s and really started to gather momentum by the mid 1980s. At that time, the business environment was very different to the one we experience today.

Business environment

In the 1980s employees were more likely to stay with one organization for many years and were recognized and rewarded for this loyalty. At the same time, organizations were relatively stable compared with today. Companies recognized for offering particular products or services would generally stick to delivering what they knew best and in the markets they were familiar with.

Same agendas

It could be said that at that time, organizations and employees had long-term agendas which were reasonably well aligned. Organizations wanted employees who stuck around and were 'company people' and employees enjoyed the stability of belonging to and growing with one organization.

The sports coaching model worked very well in this environment because this was the relationship which existed and generally still exists in sport. The sports coach and performer have similar long-term goals – a high jumper and coach, for instance, are likely to be working towards the same long-term goal, whether that is to win a local championship or achieve an Olympic gold.

Changed business environment

The business environment is now very different. Organizations have needed to become far more dynamic, offering a variety of services across a range of markets. Supermarkets in the 1980s, for instance, only sold groceries. Today they offer banking and insurance services, sell computers and even offer cell phone and internet services.

Flexibility now the key

To stay ahead, organizations now need to be highly flexible, hiring staff with specific skills to deliver new services.

Employees have realized that they can further their careers quicker in this environment by frequently moving to other organizations rather than waiting patiently for promotion in their existing company.

Different agendas

So today the agendas of employees and employers can often be quite different and are also constantly changing. Many employees will choose to align with an organization's agenda only if it also suits their own career path.

This does not happen in sport. You could not imagine a sports coach saying to their coachee: "I know you are an excellent high jumper but people are just not interested in that anymore. I need you to consider becoming a footballer because that's what people want to watch."

Likewise you would not expect a high jumper to say to their coach: "Thanks for all you've done for me but I have only been high jumping to build my jumping skills – I'm changing my career to become a basketball player."

Change in approach

Because of these changes in the business environment, you may find yourself faced with a performer who is working to a different agenda from your organization's – maybe for perfectly acceptable reasons – and so need to adapt slightly your coaching approach.

Our second dimensions take into account these potential differences of agendas at each stage of the model and allow you to explore and handle any differences without demotivating your performer.

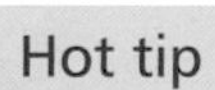

Where your coachee has a different agenda to the organization's you may need to adapt your coaching style.

Using the 2nd Dimensions

The following diagram shows our coaching process from A through to F and for each of the six stages, we have also superimposed the range of leadership styles:

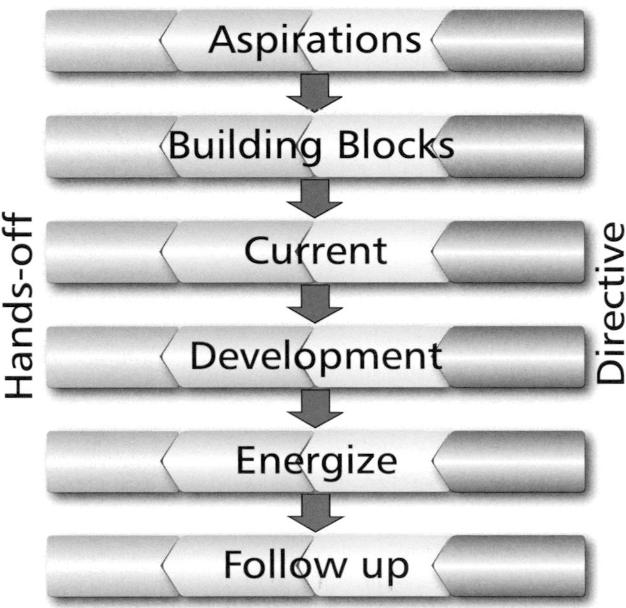

Styles for each stage

What this diagram hopefully highlights is that when we talk about introducing the second dimensions it is not just a matter of choosing one alternative coaching style to use throughout the whole process.

As we will describe throughout the rest of this chapter, at each separate stage of the coaching process (and sometimes even within each stage) you need to choose the most appropriate style to meet the specific needs at that time.

Always approach coaching on the basis of it being hands-off and only change from this if you see the need to.

Getting the balance right

To ensure the right balance, the general rule is that you should approach each stage of the coaching process on the basis of it needing to be hands-off, and only adapt towards one of the other styles should you feel there is a specific need to do so.

Ultimately, the more hands-off and empowering you keep your coaching the more responsibility you leave with your performer.

The different perspectives

By using a hands-off style you are encouraging your performer to think for themselves and are therefore working to their agenda, based on their perspectives or viewpoints.

Performer takes responsibility	You take responsibility
Performer's views	Your views
Performer's agenda	Your/organization's agenda

It therefore follows that if you decide to use a more directive or 'tell' style you are bringing into the process an element of your own agenda or perspective, or the organization's.

This may not necessarily be a bad thing, particularly if the coach and performer's perspectives are different – given our earlier explanation of the changing business environment.

Gauge the situation

When using the second dimensions, as well as focusing on the content of the coaching discussion, you need to be gauging your performer's reactions to decide the appropriate approach.

As your discussion progresses, you may decide to change your style. You may start using a hands-off style and then decide to move towards a participating/guiding style – maybe to join in with a brainstorm to stimulate the generation of new ideas.

Ask their permission

Before making such a change you can still leave the control with your performer by asking their permission to input your views, as we have previously described.

Change styles for a reason

When you change coaching styles it should be on the basis you have made a conscious decision that this is the most appropriate style for the situation. There is a big difference between choosing to use a style and sliding towards your natural leadership style just because that's the one you are comfortable with.

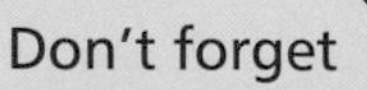

Keep the responsibility with your coachee by asking permission before providing any of your own views.

Aspirations

We are now going to focus on the detail of the second dimensions and how these are applied for each of the stages of our coaching process.

As we know, your initial discussion is around your coachee's aspirations or long term goals. In the diagram below, your coachee's perspective is represented on the left hand side as this will be the focus if your coaching style is hands-off. The right-hand side represents the organizational or business perspective which would start to be brought into the discussion if you were to move towards a directive or 'tell' style.

(We have simplified the leadership spectrum in this diagram purely to make it easier to see but we are assuming that the other intermediate styles are still there.)

Personal aspirations	Aspirations	Business vision

Organizational perspective

We have described in detail the long-term goals from the coachee's perspective so we do not need to look at this again. We do need to consider the opposite end of the spectrum which is the organization's aspirations or long-term goals. In the business context this is often referred to as the 'business vision'.

Business vision

Most successful organizations will have a business or organizational vision. This describes where the organization plans or needs to be in the future. For instance: "Our vision is to become one of the world's leading players in..."

Most organizations review this from time to time to ensure it is still valid and relevant just as your performer may decide to review their aspirations.

Aligning others to the vision

Most organizations publish their vision for the benefit of its clients, stakeholders, shareholders and also for its employees.

By making its employees aware of its vision, an organization ensures its employees are fully supportive of the vision and therefore actively aligning their thinking and actions towards helping to achieve it.

Second dimensions and your performer

If we apply this understanding of the business perspective to our coaching you will see that, of all the coaching stages, ***Aspirations*** is probably the simplest to translate into practice.

This is because you will rarely come across a situation where you need to bring in this business perspective. In this stage, probably more than in any other, it is really important to keep to your performer's agenda – that is, their personal aspirations. By keeping your coaching style to the left-hand, hands-off end of the spectrum you leave the responsibility with your performer.

Don't forget 

You will very rarely need to bring in the business perspective during your discussion over aspirations.

Demotivating

It would become very demotivating if you moved right over to the right hand side and tried to impose your organization's views i.e. its vision over your performer's own aspirations.

Likewise, you should avoid telling your performer what you believe their aspiration should be. Remember your performer's aspiration becomes the key motivator for the coaching – the 'what's in it for me' – and they are unlikely to be very motivated if you tell them they can't work towards their own aspirations.

Dealing with Differences

Different agendas

In reality, it is not very likely that your coachee's aspirations are going to be far out of line with the organization's vision. Most people join organizations they believe fit with their own values and are likely to help them to achieve their own career aspirations. Likewise, organizations tend to choose people who they believe will align with and help deliver their vision.

Hot tip 

Only consider moving from a hands-off style if there is a mismatch in the coachee's and organization's agendas.

When to change style

If your coachee's agenda and the organization's align, then there is no reason to move from a hands-off style – responsibility can remain with your coachee and there is no need for you to provide any input. This is an important principle that holds true in the application of the second dimensions for each of the stages.

Just occasionally, your coachee may express an aspiration which is not in line with the organization's. For instance, your coachee may say they ultimately want to work for a small family-run business which will allow them to be a bigger player in a smaller company. Your organization's vision may be to become the world's largest in its field. Of course, in most cases your coachee will know this already.

Small element of input

When faced with this type of situation it may help to provide a small amount of input (with their permission) to remind your coachee of the organization's vision and that they should therefore be aware that the organization is unlikely to fulfill their ultimate aspiration.

No roles available

Likewise, your coachee's ultimate role may not be one that exists in the organization or you may know that role is unlikely to become available in the organization to satisfy their timescale. Your coachee's aspiration, for example, might be to become a project manager but the organization may have a policy of outsourcing all project activity to third party project management specialists.

Beyond the organization

The long-term outcome of the above scenario is that, to fulfill their aspiration, your coachee will ultimately need to leave the organization and find a role elsewhere. This is an interesting paradox and one you may encounter from time to time.

If you do not openly discuss this issue with your coachee it won't stop them having this aspiration, it just means they will work towards it without your knowledge or involvement.

So, openly discussing it with your coachee may not change their aspiration or their eventual need to find a role in another organization. But it is a more positive stance to take because:

- During the time your coachee is with you, they are more likely to be motivated and engaged as you work positively with them towards achieving their aspiration
- The fact you are prepared to discuss and are genuinely committed to your coachee's long-term career is likely to encourage them to stay with you longer
- There is a chance an alternative solution or opportunity will present itself which your coachee can explore with you

Remember, in today's business environment few people stay with one company for many years. It is far better to work positively with them during the time they are working with you.

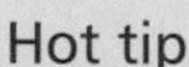

Hot tip

Even if your coachee's aspiration is not possible to achieve within the organization, encourage them to talk about it openly.

Building Blocks

Having looked at the application of the second dimensions in the context of ***Aspirations***, we can now apply many of the same principles when dealing with the next stage in the coaching process, ***Building blocks***. Let's start by looking at the two ends of the coaching and leadership styles spectrum:

Short-term goals	**Building blocks**	Business objectives

Business objectives

We know that *Building blocks* are the short-term goals which will lead to the achievement of your coachee's aspiration. Within the business context, the equivalent short-term goals are often referred to as business objectives. An organization sets business objectives which will move it towards achieving its vision.

Applying the same principles we did for ***Aspirations*** you should start your coaching based on a hands-off style so that you leave the responsibility with your coachee. Only where there is a specific reason, should you look to move to one of the other coaching styles.

Reasons to change style

Hopefully your coachee will come up with a comprehensive list of *Building blocks* which will take them a step at a time towards their aspiration. There may be a few occasions when you may need to move your coaching style more to the right on our spectrum. Here are some examples:

- Your coachee genuinely does not understand or appreciate all the things they need to achieve to get them to their aspiration
- Your coachee's chosen *Building block* is not feasible to focus on now because of business commitments or pressures relating to the achievement of the business objectives
- Your coachee responds better to generating ideas when they are able to bounce ideas off other people

We will take each of these examples in turn and look at possible ways of handling each.

Coachee doesn't know all the steps

On the face of it, the obvious solution appears to be to jump in with the other *Building blocks* that you, as an experienced manager, already know. This is an option but only if you feel that a missing ***Building block*** is going to fundamentally throw the coachee off course. It is still preferable to leave the discovery to your coachee who will eventually realize they have missed a step.

Beware

Even if your coachee doesn't come up with all the building blocks, don't necessarily tell them straight away the ones you believe they have missed.

Building block in the way of business

Here there is a mismatch between your coachee's agenda and the organization's. If the organization has a business objective to produce one thousand widgets by the end of the month and your chief widget maker – who you are coaching – decides their next ***Building block*** is to become proficient as a first line manager, finding the opportunity to come off widget making at this crucial time may be a problem.

Ahead of target

If, of course, you are ahead of your widget-making target then you may have the flexibility to let them pursue this *Building block*. If business pressures mean you cannot, you will need to discuss this with your coachee to determine whether the ***Building block*** can be adapted or if they are prepared to pursue an alternative until the short-term issue is resolved. This may mean you adopting a style which is somewhere towards the right-hand side of the spectrum.

Generating ideas

You may find your coachee prefers to work with others when brainstorming new ideas. If your coachee has taken responsibility they may ask you to join in at this point anyway.

This is an occasion where you may only need to shift your style slightly to the right to be more participating and supporting. Take care you don't then start to dominate the meeting. Only add ideas to help stimulate the discussion.

Hot tip

Sometimes your coachee may want you to join in to help stimulate their own thoughts and ideas.

Current

Now your performer has chosen the *Building block* they want to work on we move to the discussion around their current level of capability relating to this ***Building block***. Through careful questioning you will be stimulating your performer's own self-awareness which is therefore shown on the left-hand side of the spectrum for this stage.

Should you need to provide direct input to your coachee on the subject of ***Current*** it will be in the form of additional or external feedback – your viewpoint or the views of others on their current capability.

It is best if your coachee is encouraged to analyze their own capability which will help them become more self-aware.

The benefits of leaving responsibility with your performer are:

- Encouraging your performer to analyze their capability helps them to generate better self-awareness
- Only your performer can truly know how it feels performing an activity from a psychological point of view
- Your performer may disagree with or deny the feedback you provide them, especially if they don't like what they hear

Effective questioning

Through the use of effective questioning, as we described in Chapter 5, it is normally possible to help your performer create a good understanding of their own performance and capabilities.

Performer's views first

One advantage of getting your performer to give their views on their capability first is that it will provide you with a better understanding of your performer's thoughts regarding their capability.

If your performer describes in detail their lack of capability and you believe this is a correct perception, it will save you having to give them any bad news! It also means you can keep to a hands-off coaching style with little need to provide additional input.

Overly negative performer

Alternatively, if you believe your performer is being unnecessarily hard on themselves, it provides you with an opportunity to explore why they have such a negative view of their capability. This may in itself be why they are not performing at their desired level.

Overly positive performer

The more difficult scenario is where your performer expresses what you believe to be a falsely positive view of their capabilities. If they truly believe this, when you try to tell them something different, they are likely to see you as the problem rather than the issue you are trying to discuss.

In this situation it is best to use a hands-off style. Question your performer to encourage them to explore their real capabilities but be careful not to lead them into saying what you want them to say. You are just trying to get them to see themselves as they really are.

Asking your views

Your performer may ask you for your opinion or for any external evidence you have and this would be a reason to move your style towards the right-hand of our spectrum and provide some external feedback. Stick to all the guidance we have already given about providing a balance of positive and negative feedback and ensure you can back up your observations with evidence.

Hot tip

It is always preferable to get your coachee's views before deciding whether you need to provide any input.

Development

Once your coachee has explored the nature of their development gap – the difference between where your coachee believes they are and where they need to be to achieve their ***Building block*** – they will then need to come up with possible development suggestions.

Development suggestions | **Development** | Available resources

There are just a few scenarios where you may need to use a style other than a hands-off style during this part of the discussion:

- Your coachee asks you to help them brainstorm possible ideas

  Our usual guidance applies. Take care not to dominate the discussion but also try to suggest ideas you believe will match the learning style or interests of your coachee. This will mean adopting a style that is more participating and supporting.

- Your coachee runs out of their own ideas

  Before suggesting your own ideas you should, of course, ask permission first. The same guidance we have just described then still applies.

- Your coachee is not aware of the resource issues from the organization's point of view

  This last one is a little more complex and we will therefore now explore this in more detail.

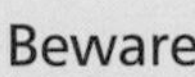

Watch your coachee doesn't come up with expensive alternatives or ones that duplicate what the organization already provides.

Standardized training

Your organization may provide certain training and development courses, workshops or materials which have been chosen because they deliver a standardized approach across the whole organization. There will also probably be cost-saving implications in providing standard solutions.

If your coachee is not aware of these options they may suggest similar solutions that duplicate what is already provided and that are also likely to cost much more to purchase on an individual basis. A small amount of input to make them aware of this is probably all that is required.

Expensive solutions

Your organization is unlikely to have a completely open-ended budget for training and development. You may even have a set budget allowance for each employee. Most development solutions resulting from coaching tend to be relatively cost-effective and sometimes cost nothing at all.

So if your coachee comes up with development ideas which are outside your organization's budgetary allowance you may, again, need to make them aware of these restrictions and ask them to consider alternative, cheaper options.

Time away from the job

Another important resource factor to consider is how much time your coachee's development is going to take out of their normal working day.

One advantage of coaching over other forms of development is that coaching solutions are normally more focused and often they can be fitted around your coachee's normal work.

Some solutions, however, may mean your coachee taking time away from their day-to-day work commitments even if only for an hour or so at a time.

Agreeable solution

Hopefully, a workable solution can be agreed between you and your coachee but there may be occasions where you need to suggest your coachee looks for alternative development solutions that will not to be so time-consuming.

You need to do this sensitively to avoid demotivating your coachee. You may feel, having stopped them from their preferred activity, that you owe it to them to come up with alternatives. It is still best, though, to encourage your coachee to find alternatives that they are then more likely to be committed to.

Don't forget

Time away from the job for training can be disrupting but many coaching solutions can be completed as part of the job.

Energize

Hopefully your performer will come up with a range of viable development solutions which are acceptable from an organizational viewpoint. You role is now to ***Energize*** your performer so they leave feeling confident they can complete their chosen actions.

You will recall there are three elements to ***Energizing***, all of which are centred around ensuring your performer is personally committed to completing their actions. This is shown on the left-hand side of our scale below:

Personal commitment	**Energize**	Help and influence

Telling won't help

It would be counterproductive to just tell your performer to be motivated. This is something that can only come from them based on their own personal commitment and will to succeed. In this sense moving to a directive or 'tell' style is unlikely to help.

However, even if your performer is highly motivated towards their actions, sometimes these can be made easier for them to accomplish with your help or influence.

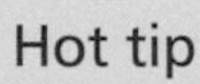

Hot tip

Sometimes, however committed your coachee is, your influence may improve their chances of success.

Your help and influence

So, whilst the right-hand end of our style spectrum is generally an area to avoid, one aspect you may want to explore with your performer is what help or influence you can bring to bear to help them avoid some of the potential blockages.

Assuming you are the coachee's manager or in a more senior position than they are, you may have the authority or influence to make things happen. For example, you may be able to:

- Persuade another manager to allow your performer to work in their department to gain the necessary experience
- Find out what project opportunities are likely to come up that your performer could become involved in
- Find extra budget allocation to finance a more costly development activity where you feel it is appropriate

Getting the balance right

There is a difference between providing help or influence to smooth the way for your performer and taking over control for making things happen. Try to find a balance such that you enable things to happen but without taking over the responsibility.

So, for instance, if you agree to talk to a senior colleague about opening up an opportunity for your performer, once you have made the connection and agreed a way forward, leave it that your performer will contact your colleague to make the final arrangements.

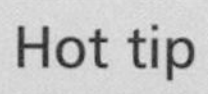

Hot tip

Try to strike a balance between providing help and taking over control.

Another way to handle this is to leave your performer with the action to make the connection and to try to make the necessary arrangements but with the option to come to you for help should they not get the desired response from your colleague.

Avoid being too helpful

Sometimes your performer needs to be left to discover things for themselves. You may think you are being helpful by giving them the answer to something or showing them where to look but if you become overly helpful your performer is not encouraged to think for themselves.

Supportive style

All of the above are examples where you are adopting a supporting style and therefore only one step away from being hands-off. Your status as manager becomes less significant as you work jointly on enabling your performer's development.

Follow up

This last stage in our process in effect represents all the subsequent meetings that will follow your initial coaching meeting. As such you may need to adopt different styles for each depending on the needs of each meeting.

On receive

Hopefully your coachee is motivated and 'on receive'. Where this is the case they will review their own performance and your style can remain hands-off.

The difficulty arises where your coachee doesn't seem to be willing to take responsibility and has not progressed their development actions. In this situation you may appear to have no choice but to start checking up on performance, moving your style to the directive end of the coaching spectrum.

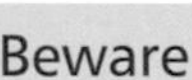

Beware

If your coachee isn't taking responsibility for reviewing their progress don't just switch to a directive style.

Before you do this, take a step back and think whether there are any alternatives to becoming directive, because to do this could undermine the whole coaching relationship and will most likely return it to a manager/subordinate footing.

Some people prefer it

In fact some people work better when they know they are being checked up on. Even just knowing that they will have to tell you about their progress when you next meet is often enough to encourage them to complete their actions.

If your performer wants this, it is something they will request. This is not the same as having to resort to monitoring or chasing your coachee's progress because of a lack of activity.

There could be a number of legitimate reasons why your coachee has not progressed their development actions including:

- Work commitments have overtaken them leaving no time to pursue their actions

  This is something which might have been possible to predict when initially energizing your coachee but at least you are now aware and can explore possible ways around it. It could mean you providing help and influence by finding ways to divert work to others so that your coachee can have the time.

- Your coachee has lost interest in pursuing this set of development actions

  All is not lost. It may be your coachee just didn't get on with their actions and you can help them explore alternatives. This is therefore still no reason to adopt a directive approach.

- Your coachee has lost interest in being coached

  This may be because they have lost sight of their aspiration or just feel the size of the development gap is too big. You can find this out through questioning and then return, at the appropriate point, to the coaching process – hopefully with renewed vigor.

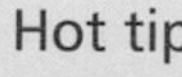

Hot tip

If your coachee has lost interest, it may be the development gap is too big. If so, break down the *Building block* to a more manageable size.

Your coachee has disengaged

This is a serious situation and may also be reflected in their day-to-day work. It is unlikely in this frame of mind that you will be able to continue coaching constructively and it may be best to just end the coaching. We will explore this in more detail in the next chapter when looking at more difficult scenarios.

Putting it All Together

If we put all of the second dimensions together you can now see the whole of the coaching process. You should also be able to see from the position of the crosses – representing example positions for your coaching style at each stage – that for one coaching session you may need to adopt a whole range of coaching styles:

Don't forget

Using the second dimensions enables you to use a range of coaching styles in one session.

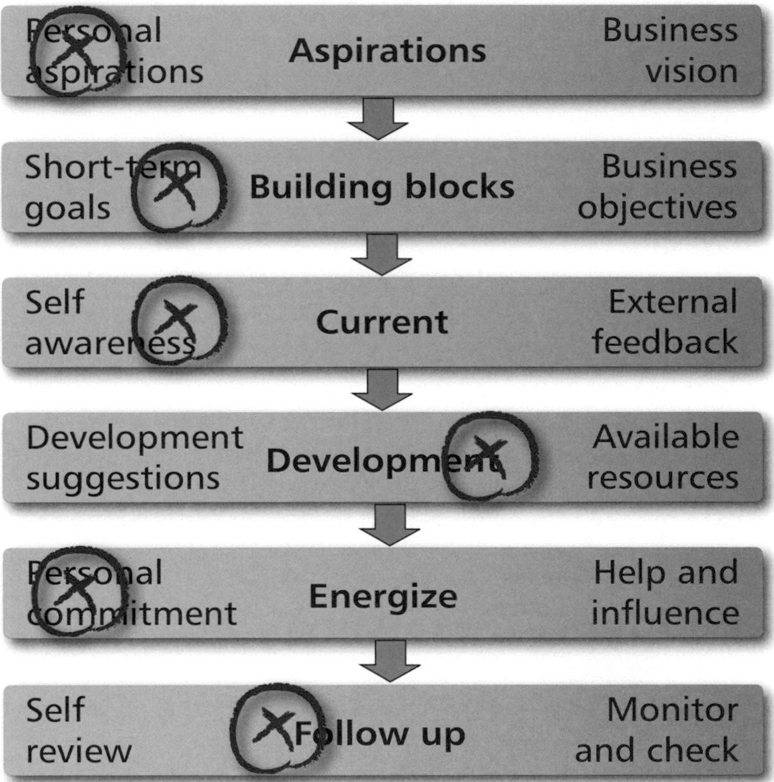

In this example you adopt a hands-off style for *Aspirations* allowing your coachee to describe their personal aspiration without needing to impose any company perspective.

Your coachee takes responsibility for coming up with their own ***Building blocks*** with just a couple of ideas from you – hence the cross is just in from the left-hand end of the scale.

You adopt a similar position when discussing ***Current*** because your coachee asks you for your opinion over one aspect of their capability.

When discussion moves on to ***Development*** your coachee comes up with a number of ideas. But they are new to your organization and are unaware of some of the internal training resources that are available which you need to make them aware of. The balance of your discussion is therefore towards a guiding style as shown.

Being new and therefore highly motivated, you are able to remain totally hands-off when working through the ***Energize*** stage with your coachee.

The only reason your style for the ***Follow up*** is not totally hands-off is because your coachee asks you for reassurance that they have been doing the right thing when you first meet. This you are able to do before returning to a hands-off style.

If in doubt

We must re-emphasize what we said at the beginning of this chapter. If you are in any doubt over applying the second dimensions then adopt a hands-off style throughout which is how we described the coaching process in Chapter 4.

Remember, even if you do incorporate the second dimensions into your coaching, you should always assume a hands-off style to begin with and only change style if there is a need which will benefit your coachee.

Don't forget

If you are in any way unsure about the second dimensions, adopt a hands-off style throughout.

Flexibility

Adding the second dimensions makes the coaching process a highly flexible one, allowing you to adapt your coaching style throughout a meeting and even within each stage to suit your coachee and the situation.

The second dimensions leave the responsibility with your coachee but still give you the flexibility to take into account the issues of your organization and the dynamics of today's business environment.

Summary

- Using a hands-off style is always preferable but the second dimensions allow you to introduce other coaching styles in a structured way
- The second dimensions are based on the leadership and coaching styles spectrum and allow the organization's perspectives to be brought into the coaching discussion
- Provided your coachee's agenda is in line with the organization's you can keep to a hands-off style which means leaving the responsibility with your coachee
- You shouldn't try to alter your coachee's aspiration even if this is not in line with the business vision although you may need to make them aware that it is not in line
- You may need to discuss how your coachee completes their aspiration beyond your organization if no roles exist
- Coaching a coachee who is ultimately going to leave to pursue their long-term aspiration can be a good way of maintaining your coachee's levels of motivation
- If your coachee's choice of ***Building block*** is difficult to pursue because of business pressures you may need to suggest to your coachee they consider an alternative
- Leaving your coachee to appraise their capability helps them to develop better self-awareness. Only provide additional feedback after seeking permission or if asked
- Your coachee's development ideas are best but they may ask you to come up with suggestions to help stimulate or supplement their thinking
- The positive side to inputting your views when ***Energizing*** is that you may be able to help or influence others to make things happen
- You may need to adopt a range of coaching styles during subsequent follow-up meetings depending on how they go
- If, initially, you have difficulty incorporating the second dimensions you can stick to a hands-off style throughout

9 Coaching Applications

Only when you start coaching will you begin to understand and appreciate the many applications of the coaching process. In this chapter we explore some of the various uses of coaching as well as looking at some of the more difficult scenarios you may face.

152 Self-Coaching

154 Mentoring

156 Business Consulting

158 More Business Consulting

160 Career Change

162 The External Coach

164 Remote Coaching

166 Bringing in Coaching

168 Embedding into the Culture

170 Difficult Scenarios

172 Some Final Tips

Self-Coaching

Throughout this book so far we have been describing the situation where you are coaching someone else. We have described the benefits of coaching and how the coach can bring an independence and challenge to a coachee's thinking. Even so, it is also possible to use the same coaching process and techniques to coach yourself. This can be particularly useful when you need to get yourself thinking in a focused way. Use the whole coaching process or just use some of the techniques when you need to think through particular issues.

Clearly, if you have the opportunity, it is better if you can ask someone else – maybe a colleague – to coach you. However, this may not be practical or there may not be anyone available who has the necessary coaching skills to help you.

Self-discipline

Coaching yourself requires a high level of self-discipline as it is important to force yourself to work through each of the stages just as you would do if you had a coach with you.

It can be very tempting to think you know the answer to something because you've thought it through before and therefore skip over an issue. Remind yourself that any previous thinking will have been done in an unstructured way and without any challenge. It is therefore unlikely to be reliable enough to use as a basis for the rest of your coaching.

Beware 

Watch that you don't base your coaching on previous thinking which may not be very focused.

Challenge yourself

Just as an independent coach will challenge a coachee, be prepared to challenge your own thinking. For instance:

- When you hear yourself using vague language
- To determine whether your aspiration is realistic
- To double-check you have thought of all the options

Using visualization

Using visualization is a great way to get clarity over your thinking. Use it, as you would with a coachee, to explore your *Aspirations*. Also try visualizing to explore all the ***Building blocks*** you need to set in place. You should be able to visualize yourself completing each ***Building block*** and so help to ensure you capture them all.

Seek external views

Without the benefit of a coach, you are reliant on your own self-awareness. It may be helpful to find someone, whose judgement you trust, to give you an honest appraisal of your current level of capability for the ***Building block*** you decide to work on.

Energizing

When *Energizing*, again, be firm with yourself and ensure you cover all three elements:

- Have the self-discipline to make your development plans SMART (or MARC)
- Challenge yourself over your levels of motivation – how committed are you to seeing them through?
- Visualize the blockages that could stop you completing your actions and determine tactics to deal with them

Driving yourself

The most difficult part of self-coaching is making sure you do what you say you are going to do. Diarize your actions and stick to your planned review date. It may help to ask a colleague to chase you over your actions.

Better still, why not encourage a business colleague or friend to look at becoming a coach as well so you can learn together and act as coaches for each other?

Hot tip

Why not try to persuade a colleague to take up coaching and you can then coach each other.

Mentoring

The term mentoring is sometimes used within different organizations to mean different things Some organizations, for instance, use the term mentoring as an alternative term for the word coaching. We are using the term mentoring here very specifically to mean:

The independent support and guidance of an individual by a trusted, more senior manager normally focusing on an individual's career development.

Often a mentor will not have any line responsibility for their mentee. Their focus is on an individual's long-term career direction and growth rather than day-to-day performance, helping them to decide their future career path and sometimes using their influence to make things happen.

Don't forget

As with coaching, the first part of mentoring involves helping your mentee to determine their future career aspirations.

Similarities

The process of mentoring therefore fits very well with the coaching process and techniques we have described in this book. Here are just some examples:

- As a mentor you will want to discuss with your mentee their long-term career aspirations
- Your relationship will most likely involve meeting up every few weeks whilst developing a long-term relationship
- You will not want to impose your views but, instead, help your mentee to determine an appropriate career path
- As a more senior player, you may be able to provide help and influence to make things happen

Responsibility

As with coaching, you should be encouraging your mentee to take responsibility for their own career decisions and development. Your style should therefore be hands-off through the effective use of open and high-gain questioning.

Working through the process

Just as with coaching, you can work through the same A-F process. The first two stages of the process, *Aspirations* and *Building blocks* are of particular relevance when mentoring, given their focus on the mentee's career direction.

Check for overlap

Once your mentee has chosen the first *Building block* they wish to work on it is advisable to check with them whether development of this *Building block* is going to overlap with any development they are pursuing as part of their day-to-day work. If this is the case, it may be best to arrange a three-way meeting to hand over responsibility for this to your mentee's line manager.

Help and influence

Another of your key roles as a mentor is to use your influence to provide opportunities for your mentee to be exposed to people and situations which they would not otherwise be able to do. Where appropriate, look out for opportunities to:

- Introduce your mentee to other senior colleagues
- Provide them with experiences which they would not otherwise get
- Enable your mentee to present their work or a special project to appropriate senior or influential players

Hot tip

As well as progressing your mentee using the coaching process you can assist them by providing opportunities for them to get exposure in the organization.

Business Consulting

An interesting and extremely useful application of our coaching process is in structuring consultancy discussions and meetings with business decision makers.

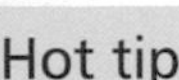

Hot tip

The coaching process also forms an ideal structure for business consulting meetings.

Rather than focussing on the personal agenda of an individual however, you are instead basing your discussion with a decision maker on the agenda and issues of the organization.

Business focus

If you recall from the last chapter we described the business equivalents of ***Aspirations*** and ***Building blocks*** which were the 'business vision' and 'business objectives' respectively. These therefore become the focus of the first part of your business consultancy discussion.

So by re-framing our original model – putting it into a business context – we have a structured process for helping a business to work through strategic issues. Let's look at the model in its business consultancy form:

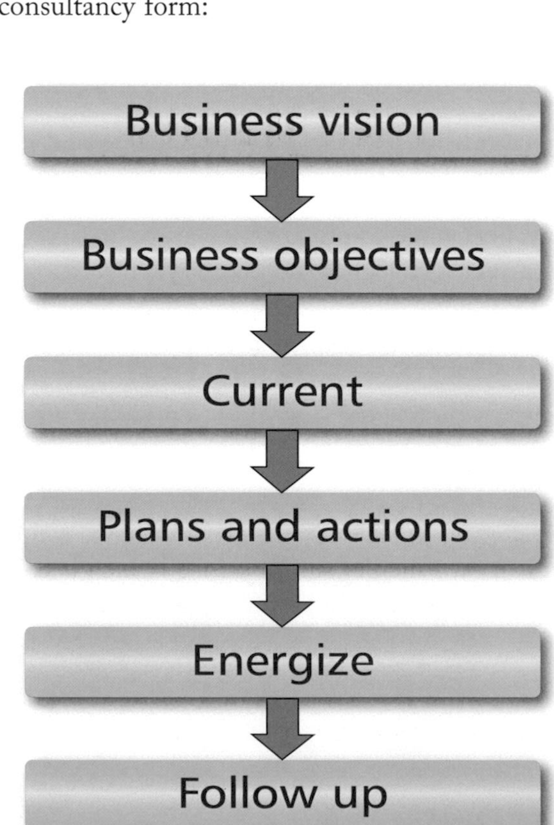

Business vision

Just as you explore ***Aspirations*** with a performer, so you can explore with your client their business vision – their long-term goals for the business. Where the organization already has this in place, it may just be a matter of reviewing this to check it is still relevant through the use of effective high-gain questions.

If an organization does not have a clear future vision statement or has one that is no longer relevant, it is preferable to hold a meeting or workshop of the key decision makers and interested players to set a new vision or to challenge their existing vision.

Determining a vision also requires a good understanding of the market and environment in which the organization operates. Just developing and communicating clear vision can make a big difference to an organization's effectiveness.

Business objectives

Once the organization has a clear vision it can determine the high-level objectives that will help it achieve this vision. As with personal ***Building blocks***, these high-level objectives can often be broken down into smaller sub-objectives which become the organization's operational objectives.

At this stage in coaching you ask your performer to choose just one or two ***Building blocks*** to work on. This does not necessarily need to be the case for an organization which may have many employees to take responsibility for delivering different objectives. However the principle of not taking on too much at once still applies so the organization does not lose its focus.

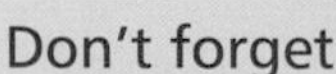

Don't forget

Unlike coaching, a business can handle a number of business objectives but still needs to remain focused.

More Business Consulting

Current

Appraisal of current performance on the chosen business objectives may be possible through discussion but may need more comprehensive analysis in order to build a full picture of the organization's capability.

At the very least you will want to look at the organization's Strengths, Weaknesses, Opportunities and Threats – or SWOT. There are more details on this and another simple analysis tool that you may want to use, PEST, in Chapter 10.

No immediate solutions

The first three stages of the consultancy process are all focussed on determining the overall direction and current capability of the organization. It is important during these stages that you do not get drawn into a discussion on possible solutions or ways forward.

Whenever the discussion strays into determining solutions, try to bring it back to the analysis. You can explain this to your client at the beginning of the process so that they are aware and don't start discussing ways forward until you are both ready to.

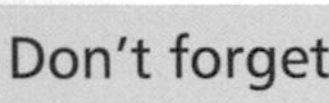

Don't be tempted to try to solve everything in the first meeting. It may take several meetings just to determine the key issues.

Separate meeting

Due to the nature of consulting it may take considerably longer than coaching to get to the point where you have jointly determined the scale and nature of the 'development gap'. It may therefore help to break the consultancy process into two stages where the initial analysis is dealt with in the first meeting and solutions are then not explored until a second or third meeting.

Responsibility

As with coaching, your role as consultant is not to take over responsibility for the issues or solutions on behalf of the organization. Your role is to help your client to better understand their business so that they can take responsibility for delivering the business improvements.

Plans and actions

In the coaching process, your coachee needed to decide their development actions. In the consultancy version these are simply substituted with the detailed business plans and actions which will help transform the organization and enable it to achieve its chosen objectives.

Energizing

Looking at the three elements within *Energizing* you will see that these are all still applicable:

1. You can still ensure all the chosen actions and plans are measurable using a model such as SMART
2. Clearly you cannot check the motivation levels of an organization in the same way you can an individual but you can explore the willingness and capabilities of its people to make it happen
3. You can explore what blockages might get in the way of the agreed business plans and determine alternative courses of action should these blockages occur

Hot tip

It is still important to *Energize* the organization using the three elements from the coaching process.

Follow up

As a consultant, you will no doubt want to develop a long-term relationship with your clients and so the follow-up meetings are a good opportunity to discuss progress. Unlike the coaching process, you should bear in mind that it could be several months between these subsequent meetings, given the time it often takes to make things happen on an organizational scale.

Scaled approach

This consultancy process, adapted from the coaching process, can be used to create structure around any business planning process. It can be used when discussing business issues with a department head or with a CEO when determining the strategic direction and business plans for an entire company.

The process remains the same but the questions and degree of analysis informing the answers just need to be scaled to fit the needs of the issue being addressed.

Career Change

An interesting coaching application is its use as a way of helping individuals make decisions over possible career changes.

Hot tip 

Most people do not get the opportunity to change careers and coaching can be a great way to help them with their career choices.

Career path

Many people's jobs or career paths come about mainly through chance or opportunity. Some individuals may have chosen to 'go with the flow' and let their careers follow directions based on opportunities as they have arisen. Others may have initially had the intention of following a particular career path only to find that opportunities have led them in other directions.

Difficulty starting again

Whatever the reason, having gone so far down a particular career path, very few people have the opportunity to completely re-think their career or even adjust it to put it back onto their original chosen path. There are a number of obvious reasons why an individual may find it difficult to change careers:

- They will have built up the knowledge, skills and experience that are specific to their current role
- They may have built up a network of contacts and friends that are helpful to them in their field of work
- They will have a salary based on their level of experience in their current role which could be difficult to match if having to start again

Time for change

There are many occasions, however, when an individual is faced with the opportunity or the need to change careers. This could be due to:

- The threat of, or actual, redundancy
- A return to work after a career break
- More financial security providing the opportunity for change
- External factors causing a re-think of their life priorities

In these situations, only the individual can decide how they want to map out their future career but it may be an ideal time to choose to do something different – perhaps to pursue a dream and try to make it a reality.

Exploring careers

You can use the coaching process very effectively to help an individual to focus and make the right career choices. You will probably need to extend the amount of time you spend with your coachee exploring *Aspirations*.

Transferable skills

Quite often an individual facing a change in their career will feel they have no choice but to look for a similar job to their last one. However, often they will have 'transferable skills' – ones that are more generic and can be used in a number of different job types.

Hot tip

Spend much longer exploring your coachee's aspirations and in particular what skills they have which could be useful in other roles.

Encourage your coachee to list their transferable skills so they can hopefully see the breadth of their experience. We have provided a list of transferable skills in the next chapter to help you.

Values and preferences

Other topic areas for discussion are your coachee's preferences and values in relation to their career. They may, for example, prefer to be creative or artistic or their preference may be working with data. Alternatively they may prefer a practical role, working with their hands or else enjoy working with people. Similarly you can discuss your coachee's values, these are things that are important to them – their rule book that governs their choices in life.

Listing your coachee's preferences and values can help them determine the types of roles and organizations they will consider.

Building blocks

Once your coachee has decided on their possible new career, you can move on to discuss the ***Building blocks*** which will help them achieve their new career. Discussing ***Building blocks*** is particularly useful at this stage to help your coachee appreciate the scale and realism of their proposed new career. Once you have these listed, the rest of the coaching can follow as normal.

The External Coach

Much of our explanation of coaching so far has centered around the internal coach – where coach and coachee both work within the same organization. Where you are a coach brought in as an external agent to provide coaching, there is no difference in the process. There are, however, one or two slight differences in the way you will need to approach your coaching in order to deal with the different relationship.

Advantages of an external coach

Here are some advantages in using an external coach over an internal coach:

- An external coach brings an independent mindset free of any of the internal organizational issues and politics
- A coachee is more likely to complete their actions and stick to agreed review dates because they may feel more reluctant to let down an external coach
- On the few occasions the external coach provides input it may be based on a broader experience and viewpoint
- There is often a perception (not always correct!) that an external coach is more experienced and capable as a coach

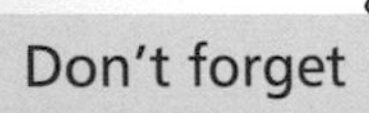

Don't forget

It is particularly important that you make your coachee feel at ease as they may not have met you before.

Starting the process

As an external coach, you may not know the coachee before you start. It is therefore critical your potential coachee is confident that you are the right person to coach them. You will need to gain their trust and build a rapport quickly.

One option is to arrange a 'getting to know you' meeting first where you can explain the relationship and discuss ground rules. You may also explore what areas they want to focus the coaching on (without getting drawn into detail). At the end of this meeting the coachee can choose whether they are happy with you as their coach or whether to seek an alternative coach.

Dressing appropriately

Be careful how you dress for your first coaching session and be mindful of its impact on your coachee – something we explored in Chapter 2. If you turn up in a suit and your coachee is dressed casually it may affect how your new coachee perceives you right from the start.

You're not their line manager

Because, as an external coach, you do not have line responsibility for your coachee you need to ensure your coachee does not over-commit to development actions such that they impact their day-to-day work. You simply need to discuss this with your coachee when *Energizing*.

Beware

If you are not their line manager be careful not to undermine your coachee's relationship with their boss.

It is important your coachee maintains a good relationship with their line manager and that it is not undermined by your involvement. Encourage your coachee to discuss their progress with their line manager and, if possible, their development actions. It may be possible that your coachee's line manager can support them with some of their actions.

Confidentiality vs. reporting back

One important consideration is whether there is any requirement by the organization to report back on progress. Clearly, where an organization is paying for the coaching, they will at least want some reassurance that their money is being spent effectively.

You may not be able to disclose the detail of your coaching sessions however, unless you have your coachee's permission. You should, at least, be able to agree to provide an outline of what area your coachee is focusing on and broadly how well they are doing.

Limited timescales

You may be limited by your contract to only providing a set number of hours of coaching. Bear this in mind when you agree with your coachee how you are going to progress the coaching. It may be better to spread the follow-up meetings to ensure your coachee has sufficient time to progress their actions.

Remote Coaching

Sometimes you may be faced with having to coach an individual remotely. This could either be because you or your performer are working away from your normal place of work or because your roles don't require a central base to work at.

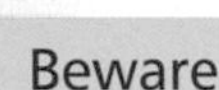

Beware

It is not advisable to try to conduct an initial coaching meeting remotely.

Not for first meetings

It is extremely difficult to conduct a first coaching meeting remotely and is not therefore something to be recommended. Without any face-to-face interaction it is very difficult to build the necessary rapport or to be able to gauge, without body language, what each other is truly communicating.

Even trying to conduct a first meeting via an online video link loses a lot of the presence gained by actually being in the room together. So, wherever possible, try to find a meeting point so that you can at least conduct your initial meeting face-to-face.

Follow-up meetings

Once you have held your first meeting face-to-face it is then possible to conduct at least some of your follow-up meetings remotely. These can be by online video conferencing (where facilities exist), telephone or by email.

Online conference

Online video conferencing is a reasonable alternative to meeting face-to-face in that you can at least see each other's faces. Depending on the quality of the equipment and the way the camera is positioned you should be able to pick up most of your performer's reactions.

Do watch the issue of privacy – check with your performer that they are on their own or their conversation cannot be overheard.

Telephone

This is the most accessible option as it is normally possible to get access to a phone wherever you are in the world. The biggest problem with using a phone is the lack of body language.

No body language

This is one of the biggest issues to deal with when not meeting face-to-face. You may be listening to what your coachee has to say but, without taking into account your performer's body language, you will only be picking up part of the whole message.

Given this, you will need to concentrate that much harder so that you can pick up any slight differences in the intonation in your coachee's voice.

If you have any doubts over the meaning behind what your coachee is saying, you should ask them to clarify. So, for example, when your coachee says: "I'm OK with that" do they actually mean they are fully behind it or are they saying that they are just about alright with it?

Limited time

Given the additional levels of concentration needed when conducting telephone meetings you will want to limit their length. It is also advisable to use the telephone for less complex discussions. So, should you find you need to start work on a new *Building block* it would be better if you could agree to meet face-to-face again rather than try to tackle it over the phone.

Online and email

There is now considerable interest in online coaching. Because of the lack of visual or verbal feedback the quality of the communication is really important. If you are just starting out in coaching it is advisable to use email just to get updates from your performer on how they are progressing with their development actions and to answer any questions they may have.

Make it happen

One problem with coaching remotely can be that either or both parties forget to keep to the agreed review dates. It is really important that you both try to maintain a momentum behind the coaching. This is something which can be discussed when *Energizing* as a potential blockage.

Hot tip 

Because of the lack of body language when using the phone, you will need to ensure you listen that much harder.

Hot tip 

Only use email as a way of informally catching up on your coachee's progress.

Bringing in Coaching

There are many benefits to bringing in coaching across a whole department or organization:

- Coaches will be working to the same process so coachees will be receiving a consistent standard of coaching
- If a coachee moves department they can continue being coached and their new manager should be able to pick up where the previous manager left off
- Coaching can enhance an organization's performance management processes
- All employees can be shown the coaching process and how, if they are coached, they can gain the most from the experience
- Coaches can support each other by coaching each other in their coaching skills and behaviors

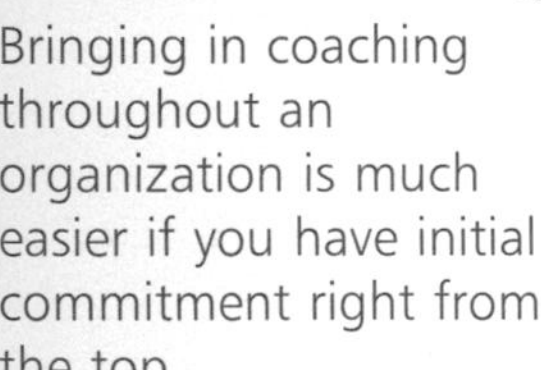

Bringing in coaching throughout an organization is much easier if you have initial commitment right from the top.

From the top

When considering bringing in coaching to a whole organization it will be far more effective if you first gain commitment from the senior management team.

Ideally you should avoid creating a two-tier system where junior and middle managers are expected to follow the coaching process and senior managers stick to traditional, inefficient development methods. This leads to friction where senior managers do not understand or support their managers using the process.

Cascading down to all levels

The most effective way to bring coaching into an organization, therefore, is to start by introducing it to the most senior managers so that they understand the process and can support their direct reports. Coaching can then be brought in systematically, cascading it down through the whole organization to managers at all levels.

On the following pages we describe a simple process that enables coaching to be brought into an organization such that everyone acting as a coach gets support from someone else.

Learning to be a coachee

Finally, even coachees can attend workshops to find out what coaching is and how they can get the most from being coached.

How the cascade works

A first group of managers learn to use the coaching process and the supporting skills such as those we have described. Probably the most efficient way to drive this through is for managers to attend a coaching skills course as a group.

When this first group of managers return from their initial training they are likely to be at a level of conscious competence based on our learning model described in Chapter 1. To move to unconscious competence they will need to practice to gain experience, something we will return to shortly.

The next group of managers now attends a coaching skills course and returns at the same stage of development as the first.

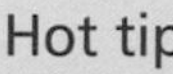

Hot tip

Using a cascade approach is a thorough way of introducing coaching to all levels of an organization.

Coaching new coaches

Those in Group 1 now coach the returning, recently-trained, managers in Group 2 to further enhance the skills and behaviors of the managers in Group 2. This process provides a number of benefits:

- Group 1 managers get the opportunity to practice their coaching skills which will help them move from conscious competence to unconscious competence
- Group 2 managers receive coaching (around the subject of their coaching skills) which will help them to focus on what they still need to develop further through coaching
- Group 2 Managers get to see Group 1 managers coaching and so can provide feedback to the Group 1 managers

Embedding into the Culture

The following shows the cascade process we have just outlined:

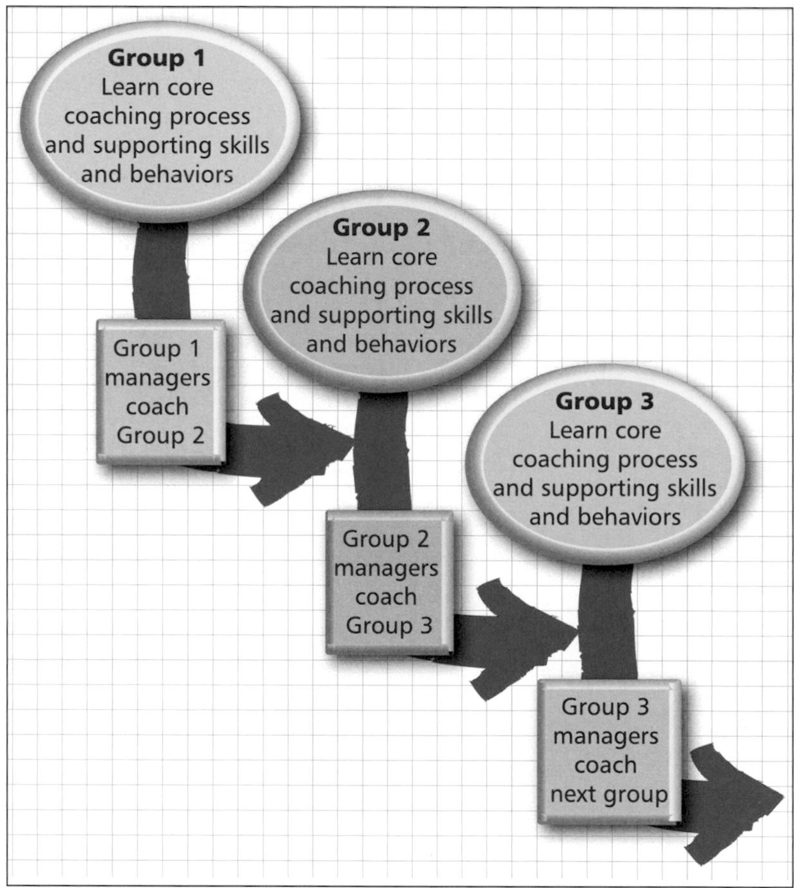

This cascade can continue with as many groups of managers as are needed. For instance, on the return of a third group, Group 2 managers can start coaching Group 3 managers and so on. This means that after learning the core skills all managers will be:

- Receiving coaching from another manager to support them and help refine their skills
- Practicing their coaching skills on another manager
- Observing a manager coaching them
- Receiving feedback from the manager they have coached on how well they felt they coached them

Finding champions

Having put a number of managers through the process we have just described, you will find that some will quickly prove to be excellent coaches (you will also find that a small number will struggle to take on coaching but more about this shortly). These excellent coaches may have picked up coaching more easily because they are already experienced in using some of the supporting skills such as questioning and listening.

Once you have identified your excellent coaches it can be useful if you can encourage them to act as coaching 'champions'. In this role they can help consolidate the coaching culture into your organization by:

- Demonstrating and encouraging best practice in coaching
- Helping and supporting others learning to coach
- Helping with more complex coaching issues or those requiring an independent viewpoint
- Acting as an expert user group suggesting new ideas and ways to integrate coaching into current processes

Hot tip

Using your most proficient managers as champions can help support the integration of a coaching culture.

Those that struggle

Just as you will find some managers who are naturally good coaches, you may find some managers struggle to apply the principles of coaching.

These may be managers who don't naturally have the skills or motivations to deal with people and team issues. This is something which may also have an impact on their general management capability and would therefore be a good subject for them to receive coaching in.

Providing extra support

You may need to provide extra support and attention for these managers – maybe through your champion coaches. In extreme cases it may be better for the managers' direct reports to be coached by someone else, at least in the short term, until they become more comfortable with coaching.

This should be treated as a last resort, however, given its potential impact on their relationship with their team members.

Hot tip

It may be possible to help managers who are struggling to get to grips with coaching by linking them up with one of your champions.

Difficult Scenarios

It may help to remind your coachee that even to stay where they are means investing in developing themselves.

1. Reluctant performer

As the saying goes... "You can lead a horse to water..." Sometimes you may want to coach a member of your team who is just not interested in their personal development or, perhaps, fears the idea of change. They may say they are completely happy working at the level they are. You will have to decide whether this will have any implications to their work and the team's.

It is worth pointing out that in today's ever-changing world, even to stand still, you have to keep developing. To accept no development can, in reality, result in going backwards.

If your performer is currently sceptical about the positive impact of coaching, it may be best to leave them for a few months so they can see the benefits achieved by others through your coaching.

2. Performer with no aspirations

Not everyone will want to commit to a long-term aspiration. Some people are what could be described as 'fatalists' and are happy to go through life letting fate take its course. Others may just find it difficult to think far into the future because of short-term issues affecting them at the moment.

You cannot force someone to think long-term. Your best bet is to push their timescale out as far as they feel comfortable going. If a short-term issue is affecting their judgement then just work to this for now. You can always come back to the issue again once the short-term issue has been resolved.

3. Performer who won't keep on track

One of the great advantages of our coaching process is that it helps an individual to focus their thinking. But not everyone will keep to the process and you may need to use all your wits to keep them on the right track.

One common example of this is when you first ask your performer to tell you about their ***Aspirations***. Let's take the scenario of a performer who wants to improve their personal organization. Here is how they might respond:

"Well I would ideally like to get to a point where my desk is far less cluttered. Because at the moment, as you have probably seen, it's a right mess. I have books and files all over the place and I can never find the thing I'm looking for..."

Here, your performer started describing their aspiration but then turned it into a description of how things are at the moment. You will need to recognise where your performer gets side-tracked and learn to carefully bring them back into the process.

Beware

Watch out for answers from your coachee that take you off the coaching process.

4. Over-ambitious performer

A performer who is over-ambitious is, in some ways, a nice problem to have. Instead of having to work at motivating them, you may need to encourage them to slow it down and take one step at a time. In a sense, the coaching process encourages this naturally but an over-ambitious performer may still try to:

- Make each ***Building block*** too big
- Tackle too many ***Building blocks*** at the same time
- Take on too many development actions
- Disregard the likelihood of blockages getting in the way

If faced with this scenario, encourage your performer through questioning to think more carefully about whether they feel their ***Building blocks*** or development actions are truly realistic.

When your performer returns for a follow-up meeting you will be able to find out if they proved to be too ambitious. If they were, this gives you something tangible to discuss with your performer. In this way, your performer will hopefully learn to self-regulate their views.

Some Final Tips

When you start coaching you will discover that there are no 'typical performers' – everyone you coach brings with them their own issues and set of circumstances – this is what makes coaching so fascinating.

You will very quickly find your own ways to deal with the more demanding situations and performers such as those just described. Here are a few final tips to help you when you start out.

Don't 'pigeonhole'

After you have coached for a while you may start to come across performers' issues that you think you have seen before or, at least, ones that seem similar. It is all too easy to think: "Here's another one of these types of problem – I know how to deal with that." If you start thinking like this there is a danger you will push your new performer to follow the same coaching solutions as the last.

Look for the differences

Remember, everyone is different. Their issues are very unlikely to be exactly the same. They will also have their own views on how they want to handle them. When coaching someone for the first time, keep an open mind and develop a way of thinking where, instead of looking for similarities between this and previous scenarios, try looking for the differences.

Hot tip

Learn from those you coach – it is amazing what you can learn. And, finally, of course, enjoy the experience!

Learn from your performer

Although you are the coach, you will be getting your performer to do most of the talking. You will find yourself hearing about a fascinating range of different life and work experiences from those you coach. You will learn so much from what you hear which you can use as part of your own development.

10 Next Steps

Having learned about the techniques and skills of coaching you now need to determine your next steps in terms of your further development as a coach and your plans to start coaching. This last chapter helps by pointing you in the direction of some useful resources.

174 What Next?

176 Coach Yourself

178 Coaching Process

179 Development Actions Log

180 Development Actions List

181 Simple Analysis Tools

182 Transferable Skills

183 Values

184 Author's Website

185 Other Useful Websites

186 Further Reading

What Next?

We have now taken you through all the essentials of coaching and hopefully given you enough of an understanding of the process, skills and behaviors for you to feel confident about starting to coach others.

Once you start coaching you will soon realize that it is a huge topic and one in which you will never stop learning new ideas and techniques. In this last chapter we provide some suggestions about how you can continue to develop your coaching skills beyond this book.

Conscious competence

You will recall from the skill development model we described in Chapter 1 that gaining an understanding of what is required on a subject moves you from *unconscious incompetence* to *conscious incompetence*.

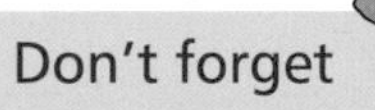

Don't forget

To get to a point where you are able to coach naturally you need to put in a lot of practice.

Hopefully, if you have been trying out some of what you have read in this book, you may have already moved towards *conscious competence*. Only through practice and experience will you get to a point where you are *unconsciously competent*.

Some of the additional ideas and resources we provide in this chapter will hopefully help you on your way.

Getting help from others

You will see on pages 176-177 that we have suggested some questions for you to ask yourself and so, effectively, coach yourself to develop your coaching skills further.

It is far better, however, if you can use others to support you while you are developing your coaching skills. Even if they aren't experienced coaches themselves it is still useful to have someone else to help you, if only as someone to test out new skills on such as questioning and listening.

Practice before the game

No professional sports person uses a real competition or match to practice new skills. They will do this in the weeks leading up to the game. The same should apply with your coaching. Don't wait until you are faced with a real coaching session to practice your skills for the first time. Here are some practice suggestions:

- Practice coaching on a friend using a non-business topic
- Role-play a business topic with a colleague
- Rehearse in front of a mirror
- Record yourself while using a voice recorder or video camera

Beware

Never use a live coaching session as a chance to practice. Find ways to practice off-line first.

Choose your first performer

When you do come to coach for the first time, choose your performer carefully so that:

- They are not likely to present you with a really complex first issue to have to deal with
- They are not likely to be over critical if things don't go exactly to plan (although some genuine feedback would be useful)
- There is not likely to be an issue over why they were picked to be coached over someone else

Hot tip

When first starting to coach, don't pick your most challenging team member. Pick someone who you feel will provide a less complicated first session.

Learn from your experience

Whether or not your first session goes exactly to plan, allow yourself some time afterwards to reflect and learn from the experience. If necessary, give yourself some follow-up coaching and determine what changes, if any, you need to make to your own development actions.

Coach Yourself

Hot tip

Use these questions to help focus your mind on what steps you need to take to become an excellent coach.

On the next two pages you will find a series of questions which you can use to coach yourself. They have been specifically written to focus your thinking on how you can aspire to become the coach that you want to be. As well as providing a prompt to get you thinking further about your coaching skills it also provides an example of the types of questions you can ask in your coaching sessions:

Aspirations

- What are your long-term aspirations in terms of coaching?
- How would you like to see yourself using coaching ultimately?
- Imagine, some time from now, when you are coaching as you would want to – describe to yourself what you're doing, what it feels like and how the coaching session is going
- How far into the future are we talking?
- How realistic is this?

Building blocks

- List on a piece of paper or white board (use a mind-map if it helps) all of the *Building blocks* which are the stages you need to achieve to get you to your vision in terms of coaching success
- Do any of your *Building blocks* need breaking down to smaller more achievable blocks?
- If you achieve all of these *Building blocks*, will they get you to the point where you achieve your *Aspiration*?
- If not, what additional *Building block* will get you there?
- Now, based on the most appropriate priorities (which we listed on page 53) which *Building block* or blocks do you want to tackle first?
- If it isn't SMART, how can you make it SMARTer?

Your focus should now be on your chosen *Building block* which, when you have achieved it, will take you one step closer towards your overall coaching *Aspiration*.

Current

- How would you describe your current level of capability in terms of this *Building block*? (Make sure you provide a balance between the positive and negative)
- Now rate yourself on a 1 to 10 scale
- Describe in detail what your score represents

Development

- Given what you know about your *Current* level and the reasons for this, what development actions could help to close the gap?
- Is there anything else that would help?
- What else could you do? (remember to keep repeating these!)
- Which ones do you think you should start with?

Energize

- Which of these actions are realistic for you to take on?
- Score each one on a 1 to 10 scale in terms of how motivated you are about completing it
- Are any below 5? – If so why are they still on your list?
- If they are not SMART, how can you write them in a SMARTer format?
- Visualize yourself completing your actions and note any potential blockages that could get in the way of you completing them
- What measures can you put in place to give yourself the best chance of completing your actions?
- When will you review your progress? Who with?

Note from all of the above that on no occasion have we needed to resort to giving you any advice. These are all questions to get you thinking about your best way forward.

Regrettably there can't be anyone with you to follow up once you have tried these first actions so now it's over to you!

Don't forget

Try to come up with as many development actions as you can. Don't stop when you just have one or two.

Coaching Process

Here is a diagram showing the full coaching process. Keep it by the side of you when you first start coaching to remind you of each of the stages.

An online, printable version is also available on the author's website – details of where to find this and other useful documents are given later in this chapter.

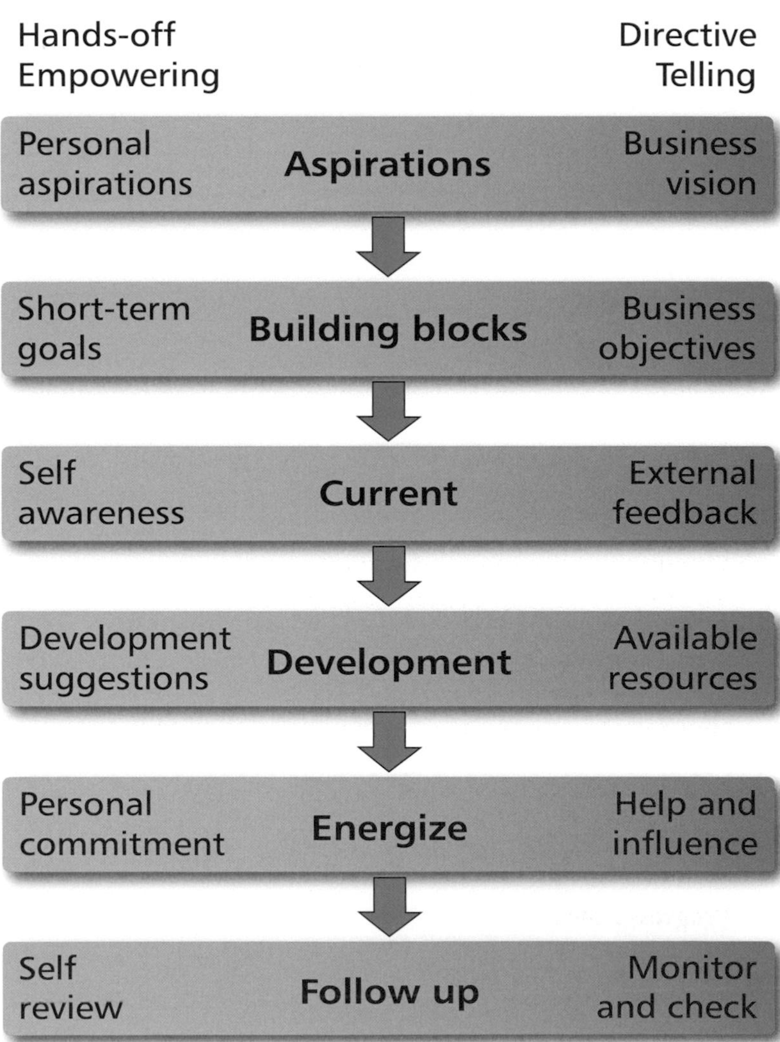

Development Actions Log

Here is a sample action plan to give your performer so they can record their chosen development actions and record their progress:

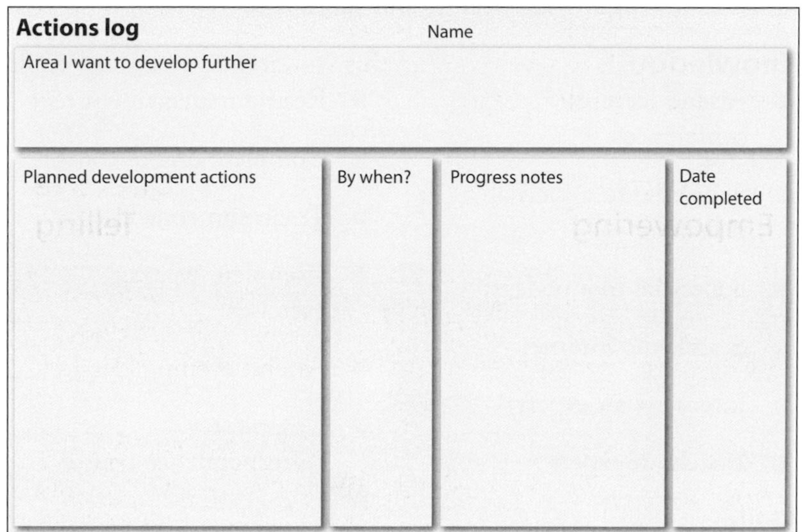

Actions log Name

Area I want to develop further

Planned development actions	By when?	Progress notes	Date completed

Remember that it is best for your performer to complete this action log so that they record their actions using their own words and are therefore more likely to take responsibility for them. The language used does not use the terminology from our coaching process so here is an explanation of how it relates:

- **Area I want to develop further**
  This is your performer's chosen ***Building block***. This should preferably be written in a SMART or equivalent format.
- **Planned development actions**
  These are the ***Development*** actions that your performer has chosen to tackle to achieve their ***Building block***.
- **Progress notes**
  These can either be completed by your performer before your next ***Follow up*** meeting or during the meeting itself.

Encourage your performer to keep these logs in a personal development folder to remind them what they have agreed to do. Each time your performer decides on new actions they can add them to their log. Over time your performer will build up a file of these logs and so keep a track of their overall progress.

Hot tip

Recording development actions is a good way to keep a check on progress towards your coachee's chosen *Building block*.

Development Actions List

In Chapter 4 we explored a few of the development ideas which your coachee could consider to help them achieve their chosen *Building block*. Here are few more ideas divided into those more suited to developing knowledge and skills:

Knowledge

- Attend lectures/ conferences
- Subscribe to a journal/ magazine
- Subscribe to a podcast
- Search the internet
- Interview an expert
- Watch an expert
- Read a management text
- Complete online courses
- Teach someone else
- Complete 'in-tray' exercises
- Attend evening classes
- Complete a correspondence course

Skills

- Role-play with a colleague
- Practice with a camcorder
- Take on a related project
- Take responsibility in the given area
- Do it with an expert watching
- Try using skills on friends
- Get someone to shadow and observe you
- Use written exercises first
- Just do it!
- Try copying someone else
- Keep repeating each small stage until comfortable
- Practice with a mirror

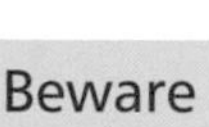

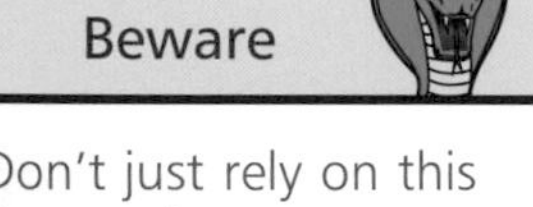

Don't just rely on this list. Make sure you get your coachee to think creatively so they come up with their own bespoke solutions.

More focused solutions

The above lists are only pointers to stimulate your coachee to come up with more focused ideas, specific to their particular issue. Hopefully they will find actions which are original, relevant and very specific to their needs.

Behaviors

We haven't listed actions related to behaviors because their chosen actions are going to be very specific and dependent upon the underlying issues driving your coachee's behaviors.

Simple Analysis Tools

Here are the business analysis tools we referred to in the last chapter. Both can be completed directly with your client but are particularly effective when completed as an exercise with a number of stakeholders such as board members, shareholders, staff and even clients. This range of different perspectives of the organization can be very enlightening.

SWOT

SWOT stands for Strengths, Weaknesses, Opportunities and Threats and under each of these four headings we have shown some typical responses for an organization:

STRENGTHS	WEAKNESSES
• Financial strength • Small size = flexibility • Exciting new product range • Well-trained staff • Loyal client base	• Sales team thinly spread • Products not proven • No succession plan • Decision-making slow • Product base too broad
OPPORTUNITIES	**THREATS**
• International market growing • Market leader struggling • Planned advertising campaign • Good media interest • Possible joint venture	• New company entering market • Cost of borrowing rising • Loss of staff to competitors • Exchange rate fluctuations • Regulation tightening

SWOT is a simple but effective way of getting a snapshot of the current state of an organization.

PEST or STEP

PEST stands for Political, Economic, Social and Technological. Our example again shows the types of topics and responses that can be added to each of the four areas:

POLITICAL	ECONOMIC
• Current/future legislation • Regulation • Government policy • Trade agreements • Lobbying groups	• Home/international market • Taxation • Interest rates/Exchange rates • Market/seasonal/trade cycles • International trade issues
SOCIAL	**TECHNOLOGICAL**
• Demographics • Consumer attitudes/fashion • Ethical/environmental trend • Lifestyle changes • Media interest	• IT development • Product development • Access to new technologies • Intellectual Property issues • New distribution channels

PEST is another useful exercise which focuses on the market and environment in which an organization operates.

Transferable Skills

Hot tip

Use the lists on these two pages when discussing possible future career options with your performer. They may want to take them away and think about them before you have your next meeting.

In Chapter 9 we described how it can be useful, when coaching someone who is considering a career change, for them to list all their transferable skills. Transferable skills are those that can be utilized in a number of careers or roles. It can be difficult to think of these without prompting so here is a list of the more common ones with a couple of spaces to add some more:

- Leading others
- Making decisions
- Completing jobs
- Improvising, adapting
- Co-ordinating others
- Managing budgets
- Listening
- Coaching
- Selling
- Negotiating
- Presenting
- Testing
- Delegating
- Training
- Problem solving
- Generating new ideas
- Adapting existing ideas
- Building/constructing
- Managing projects
- Understanding clients

- Working within a team
- Counseling
- Motivating others
- Researching
- Gathering information
- Organizing information
- Analyzing information
- Fixing and repairing
- Problem solving
- Developing others
- Thinking strategically
- Dealing with people
- Dealing with numbers
- Creative writing
- Business writing
- Strategic visioning
-
-
-
-

Values

Similarly, it can be a useful exercise for your performer to catalogue their personal values – the things that are important to them and which drive their internal decision-making. These form the 'rule book' for all of our choices.

Again, here is a list of common values to prompt your performer:

- Flexibility
- Openness
- Honesty
- Recognition
- Money/wealth
- Individuality
- Responsibility
- Professionalism
- Challenge
- Care for others
- Risk
- Routine
- Empowerment
- Security
- Status
- Perfectionism
- Personal growth
- Contact with people
- Health
- Trust

- Family
- Work/life balance
- Variety
- Travel
- Love
- Pressure
- Experience
- Tradition
- Friendship
- Achievement
- Power
- Creativity
- Rules
- Independence
- Competition
- Respect

Author's Website

Hot tip

Versions of some of the main documents in this book are available for you to print off here.

You can get free access to the main coaching documents and forms from this book directly from my own website. You can download and print off copies of your most needed documents for use in your coaching sessions and find additional coaching hints and tips. The website address is:

- *http://www.stepchangedevelopment.com/ourservices/coaching/resources/resources.html*

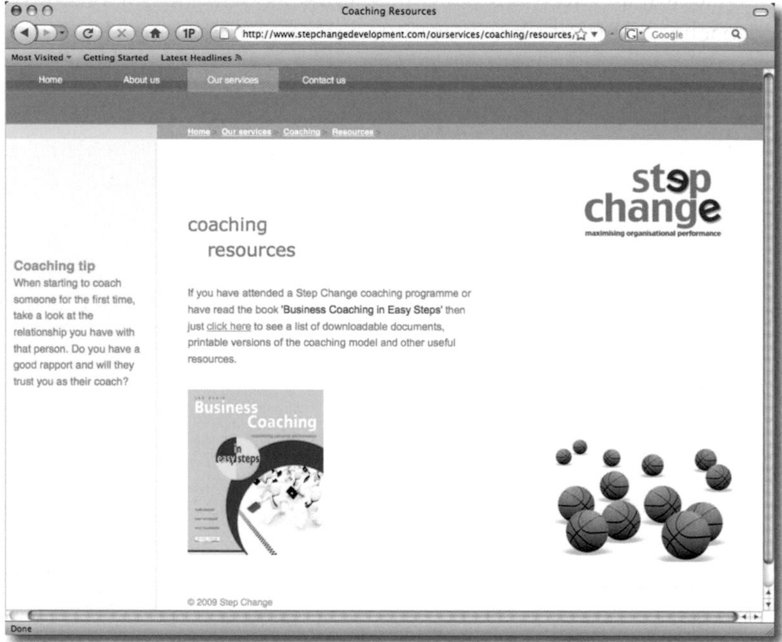

This website is updated with new material from time to time. Examples of what you can access include:

- A printable version of the coaching process diagram
- A printable version of the development actions log shown earlier in this chapter
- Case studies for you to use to practice your coaching skills with a colleague
- A self assessment questionnaire to determine your dominant coaching style – something you can also ask your team to complete to get their views

Other Useful Websites

As you can imagine, if you search under 'Coaching' on the internet, there are literally thousands of related websites. Here is a selection which contains some interesting material on coaching and some of the key supporting skills:

Coaching

- *http://www.wabccoaches.com/*

  This is the site for the Worldwide Association of Business Coaches, an international professional association for business coaches. This site has some interesting coaching articles.

- *http://www.associationforcoaching.com/pub/pub07.htm*

  This site provides a number of free coaching articles with this particular page focussing on coaching in an organization.

Body language

- *http://www.bodylanguageexpert.co.uk/*

  This site provides some interesting articles on a range of issues relating to body language including the issue of cross-cultural differences

General

- *http://www.changingminds.org*

  This is a great website which provides an overview on a whole range of skills, techniques and models including the Myers-Briggs Type Indicators or MBTI we mentioned in Chapter 6.

- *http://www.businessballs.com*

  Again, another great generalist website providing free training exercises and background information on some of the standard management and business models and theories.

Leadership

We have referred in this book to the concept of using different styles of leadership. Most sites relating to this subject have a heavy commercial emphasis. One of the best sites to pick up background information on the subject is:

- *http://en.wikipedia.org/wiki/Situational_leadership*

Further Reading

Here is a selection of books for further reading. These books provide different perspectives on the subject of coaching and some of the supporting knowledge, skills and behaviors we have explored:

- *The Tao of Coaching* by Max Landsberg (Profile Books). This book tackles coaching from a different angle by taking you through a journey of discovery with a fictional manager called Alex. This is a relatively quick and easy read and reinforces many of the messages about the essential skills and behaviors of a good coach.
- *Coaching for Performance* by John Whitmore (Nicholas Brealey Publishing). Originally published in 1992, this is still probably one of the most well-respected books on coaching and emphasizes the empowering role of the coach.
- *The Inner Game of Tennis* by W. Timothy Gallwey (Pan Books). This book was probably one of the earliest to create a cross-over from sports psychology into the business environment. There are now a number of books in the series all focusing on the impact of the mind on our performance.
- *Techniques for coaching and Mentoring* by Megginson & Clutterbuck (Elsevier). A practical book with some very useful techniques backed up by some realistic case studies.
- *The One Minute Manager* by Blanchard and Johnson (Harper Collins). This is another quick book to read – only 112 pages – and focuses on three simple yet effective management techniques, each of which only takes just one minute.
- *One Minute Manager Meets the Monkey* also by Blanchard (Harper Collins). This is another book in the series with a very unusual title. All becomes clear when you read it! It provides some useful management techniques to encourage those that work for you to take personal responsibility.
- *The Definitive Book of Body Language* by Allan and Barbara Pease (Orion Books). Allan Pease has been writing books on body language for many years and is also a renowned speaker on the subject. This provides a comprehensive and fascinating guide to all aspects of body language in business and social contexts.

Index

A

Action log. *See* Development action log
Action plan 159
Advice 25
Agendas 131
  Aligning 136
  Different 131, 136
Analysis Tools 181
Application
  Direct 111
  Indirect 111
Aspirations 46–49, 92, 134–135, 176
  Benefits 48
  Changing 117
  Finding 47, 49
  In second dimensions 134
  Making SMART 97
  Visualizing 106
Assertiveness 15
Athletes 8
Attention 36
Auditory 102
Author's website 184
Awareness
  Raising 70
  Self-awareness 8, 54, 140

B

Balanced view 57, 110
Basketball coach 9
Behaviors 14
Benefits 28–29, 30
Best practice 169
Blockages 63, 98
  Self 64
  World 64
Body language 38, 80–81, 82, 165, 185
  Eye contact 81, 86
  Facial feedback 81
  Lack of 165
  Nodding 80
  Taking notes 81
Bottom-line improvement 28
Brainstorming 58, 77, 88–89, 139
Budget 143
  Finding extra 144
Building blocks 50–53, 115, 176
  As goals 92
  In second dimensions 138–139
  Interrelated 53
  Listing them all 52, 139
  Making SMART 97
  Prioritizing 53, 61
  Recording 87
  Too big 51
  Visualizing 106
Business
  Benefit 29
  Consulting 156–159
  Direction 158
  Dynamics 149
  Objectives 138, 157
  Perspectives 134
  Pressures 138, 139

C

Cafés & restaurants 35
Camcorder 59
Career 18
  Break 160
  Change 160
  Choice 161
  Direction 154
  Preferences 161
Cascade approach 166
Case studies 184
Challenging 8, 11, 25, 47, 153
Champions 169
Chasing 146
Chat show hosts 73
Checking up 146–147
Chipping away the bits 77
Clarify 83
Coach
  As manager 10
  External 162–163
  In sport 130
  Role of 8, 25
  Skills of 11
Coachee. *See* Performer
Coachee workshops 166
Coaching
  Applications 18–19, 152–172
  Benefits 11, 27, 28–29, 40
  Bringing in 162, 166–167

Concluding 31, 121
Embedding 168
In business 10
In sport 8
Introducing 40, 162
Ongoing 110–126
Out of the organization 137
Preparation 40
Remote 164–165
Self 152–153, 176–177
Starting 30
Coaching process 44–68, 178
Coachee learning it 45, 166–167
Familiarity with 45
Coaching relationship 24–32
Coaching styles 12–13, 128, 132–133
Appropriate style 13, 136, 138
Directive 12
Dominant 13
Hands-off 12, 136
Right balance 132
Colleague, using 153
Coming off-track 44
Commitment from the top 166
Communication 38–39
Competence 20–21, 174
Compromise 29
Concentration 82
Confidence 11, 15, 27
Confidentiality 25, 40, 87, 119, 163
Conflict of interest 26
Consciousness 21
Consistency 17
Control, taking 25, 89, 145
Convergence 76
Conversational, keeping it 74
Corridor coaching 119
Counseling 17
Creativity 13, 129
Crisis 16
Culture 168
Current 54–55, 177
Business consulting 158
In second dimensions 140–141
Reviewing 112

D

Delegating 12
Delegation 18
Demotivating 13, 135, 147
Desired level 54
Desks 39
Detail 56–57
Development 58–59, 177
Actions 59, 180
In goal setting 92, 107
In second dimensions 142–143
Development action log 87, 179
Completing 87
Development gap 54, 142, 158
Too big 147
Differences 136–137, 172
Difficult scenarios 170–171
Directive style. *See* Leadership styles
Disruptive behavior 17
Distinctive phrases 84, 86
Distractions 34, 36
Divergence 77
Doubt 149
Dreams 50, 160
Dress 38, 162
Drinking 19

E

Elitism 30
Email 165
Empowerment 27, 121
Energize 62–63, 153, 177
Business consulting 159
In goal setting 92
In second dimensions 144–145
Environment 34, 38, 130–131
Environment, business 10, 130
Evaluation 31, 122–123
Keeping it simple 31, 124
When to evaluate 123
Evidence 57
Experience 21
Explaining
Responsibility 24
Roles 24

F

Face-to-face 164
Failure 9, 27, 105
Familiarity 45
Fatalists 170
Feedback 57, 125

Feeling 103
First meeting 37, 40–41
Flexibility 128, 131, 149
Focus 8, 11, 16, 53
  Through questioning 76–77
Focussed development 16
Focussed thinking 152
Follow up 66, 118–119, 164
  Business consulting 159
  In goal setting 92
  In second dimensions 146–147
Further reading 186

G

Garbage in, garbage out 25
Gauging the situation 133
Goals 10, 92, 98
  External influences 98
  Imposing 27
  Measurable 95
  Poorly set 93
  Reactions to 98
  Realistic 95
  Reviewing 96
  Setting 93
Goal-setting 92–108
  Examples 106–107
  Models 94
Going backwards 112
Golf 29
Ground rules 40, 162
Group learning 17
Guiding 12

H

Habits 15
Hands-off style. *See* Leadership styles
Hawthorne effect 124
Help 144, 174
Honesty 25
Hotels 35

I

Ideas 75, 139, 143
Images, in mind 103
Improvement 112
  Recognizing 67
Incompetence 21–21
Influence 144, 155
Influencing 15
Input, providing 136
Inspiring 100–101
Instructing 9, 12
Interrupting 49, 73
Interruptions, managing 36

J

Jacket exercise 61
Judging 47, 118

K

Keeping on track 31, 41, 44, 171
Kinesthetic 102–103
Knowledge 14, 16
  Group learning 17
  Learning knowledge 17
  Underpinning 60, 111

L

Language 104
  Vague 76, 153
Leadership styles 12–13, 128–129, 132
  Directive 16, 39, 132
  Getting the balance right 132
  Hands-off 12, 24, 129, 132
Leadership styles spectrum 12–13, 128–129
Learning levels 14
Learning opportunities 110
Learning stages 20–21
Learning styles 60
Learning to drive 14, 20–21
Life priorities 160

Line manager 163
Listening 79
  Active 83
  Barriers 82
  Filtering 82
  Practicing 59
  Reasons for 79
Location 34, 35
Long term solution 13, 15
Losing interest 147
Lowering sights 117
Loyalty 130

M

Manageable chunks 50
Management style 39
Manager as coach 26
Managing meetings 18
Manipulation 75
MARC 94, 96
Measurement tools 31
Meeting rooms 34–35
Mental blocks 114. *See also* Blockages
Mentee 155
Mentoring 154–155
Mentor, role of 154
Mind mapping 88–89
Mindset 9
Mirror, practicing with 175
Monitoring 12
Motivation 27, 62–63, 75
Myers-Briggs Type Indicator 99

N

Negative thinking 105, 141
Negotiation 19
Next meeting 65
Non-verbal communication. *See* Body language
No, in response to questions 71
No suitable roles 137
Notes
  Observation 125
  Storing 87
  Taking 37, 59, 86–87

O

Objectives 29
Observer, using another 125
Observing 125
Office layout 39
Office, your 34
Online video 164
On receive 24, 30, 146
Open-minded 24
Openness 25, 41, 137
Opinions, your 56, 141
Opportunities 158
Optimism 67
Outcomes 17, 31, 97, 114
Ownership of the process 45, 87

P

Paraphrasing 83, 84
Participating 12
Passing to another manager 120
Perception 141, 162
Performance improvement 11
Performer
  Ambitious 171
  Choosing 30, 175
  Disengaged 147
  Getting to know 162
  Highly critical 56
  Negative 141, 170
  Perspective 30
  Positive 56, 141
  Reluctant 170
  Role of 40
  Singling out 30, 175
  Typical 172
Permission 57, 61, 133
Personal development folder 179
Personal growth 28
Personality 99
Personality types 99
Personalized solutions 11
Personal objectives 29
Personal organization 15, 19, 106, 171
Perspectives, different 133
Pessimism 67
PEST 181
Pigeonholing 172
Plans, changing 114

Poor performance 17
Positive thinking 105, 141
Practice 45, 175
Praise 8, 114
Preparation 34–42
Presentation skills 60
Privacy 34, 119, 164
Probing 78
Professional study 59
Progress
  Reviewing 65, 110, 116
  Slow 113
Progress notes 179
Promotion 26, 28, 131
Psychology 9, 140
  In counseling 17
  Personality 99

Q

Questioning 15, 49, 55, 70, 140
  Keeping conversational 41, 74
Questions 72
  Assumptive 74
  Closed questions 71
  High-gain 72–73, 111, 154
  Leading 74, 75, 141
  Open questions 71
  Preparing 41
  Probing 78
  Reasons for 70
  Sensitive 75
  The question 'why?' 78, 113
  Using 'tell me' 78

R

Raising the bar 117
Rapport 41, 162
Reading, further 186
Redundancy 160
Re-energizing 113
Reflecting 84
Relationship 10, 15
  Building 26
  Ongoing 15, 120–121
Relaxed 34, 39, 41
Repeating stages 45
Replaying words 84
Reporting back 163
Resistance 27, 29
Responsibility 11, 27, 66, 154, 158
  Handing back 129
Role of coach 8, 24
Role of performer 24
Role playing 59, 175
Running over time 37
Rushing 36

S

Scale, 1 to 10 55, 56, 63
Seating arrangements 38
Second dimensions 128–150
  Aspirations 134–135
  Building blocks 138–139
  Current 140–141
  Development 142–143
  Energize 144–145
  Follow up 146–147
  Using 132, 148–149
Self assessment 27, 184
Self-awareness 54, 140
Self-discipline 152
Selling 12
Selling skills 15, 19, 28
Senses 102
Silence 49, 73
Six-step process 44
Ski instructor 9
Skill-base 28
Skills 14
SMART 94–95, 96–97, 153, 179
  And visualizing 101
  Derivations 96
  In sport 100–101
Smell 102
Smoking 19
Solutions 60–61, 143
Solutions, long term 15
Sounding board 8
Staff rooms 34
Standardized training 142
Standing still 170
Staying on top 8
Strategic thinking 15
Strategy 156
Strengths 55, 158. *See also* SWOT
Sub-goals 52, 92
Success 31
  Celebrating 67, 115

Summarizing 83, 84
  Examples 85
Support 169, 174
Supporting 12, 70–90, 145
SWOT 181

T

Taste 102
Telephone 165
Telling 9, 144
Tell me, use of 78, 106
Territory 34
Thinking
  Creative 11
  Traditional 77
Thinking styles 103
Threats 158, 181
Time away from the job 143
Time keeping 36
Time management 15
Timescales
  Agreeing 65
  Career 137
  Limited 163
Timing 37, 65
Trainers, sports 9
Training costs 142
Training courses 15, 16, 58
Transferable skills 161, 182
Transfer to the workplace 111
Trigger words 102
Trust, lack of 26
Twenty questions 71

V

Value, adding 25
Values 161, 183
Video conferencing 164
Vision 134
  Aligning to 135
Vision, business 134, 157
Vision statement 157
Visual 102
Visualization 101, 102–103, 104–105, 153
Voice recorder 175
Voice, tone of 38

W

Watch, referring to 36, 81
Weaknesses 55, 158. *See also* SWOT
Websites 184–185
WIIFM 30, 48
Work commitments 143
Work/life balance 15, 29, 31

Y

Yawning 81
Yes, in response to questions 71